GADGETS AWAY

100

GREAT GAMES
TO PLAY

FIONA JENNISON

summersdale

GADGETS AWAY

An Hachette UK Company
www.hachette.co.uk

Summersdale Publishers Ltd
Part of Octopus Publishing Group Limited
Carmelite House
50 Victoria Embankment
LONDON
EC4Y 0DZ
UK

www.summersdale.com

Printed and bound in Poland

ISBN: 978-1-78685-244-1

Substantial discounts on bulk quantities of Summersdale books are available to corporations, professional associations and other organisations. For details contact general enquiries: telephone: +44 (0) 1243 771107 or email: enquiries@summersdale.com.

Dedication

Many kisses to those who I can't kiss any more. My mother Arlene, my sister Amanda, and Ralph. May you three be dancing on water somewhere.

Ginormous thanks to Daddy Big, John Jennison, easily the best dad in the world.

Marieke Schoenmaeckers, a huge thank you for your input and friendship.

Olivia, I love you to Pluto and back, especially for your patience while Mummy was writing.

Hugs to my brothers Eeko and PJ and their girls Ana and Simone. Thanks to Diane Ferrier, Jane Gerber, Niamh O'Sheehan, Steve Hughes, Pete Hodges, Leslie Dewhurst, Cath and Nigel Atkins, Pod Blumen and Joanna Lee for all your support.

Finally big kisses to my inspirational young friends Belle, Pippa, Paula, Laia, Noa, Mario, Roisin, Summer, Oscar, Arun, Stan, Nancy, Africa, Desy, Layla, Evie, Xander, Lua and Paula P.

CONTENTS

INTRODUCTION

So, why should you buy this book or thank your friend who bought it for you?

This book is for parents who are sick of seeing their children glued to a screen; families both big and small who want to learn new games or be reminded of the great games we played before the invasion of the iPads.

Gadgets Away has super-simple games for when the bambinos need a quick distraction.

Other games are more involved to get the whole family or friends having fun together: giving those tablets a break, before they actually break…

Some of the games are invented, some come from teaching ideas, some are British classics, others are international classics and the rest are the best gems from the internet.

After the first introduction, your sidekicks will almost certainly play these games on their own for weeks on end (proven!) so the teaching of the games is time well spent…

The games have been selected for their fun factor and for their ease to organise – you only need things you would normally have at home. Cheap as chips.

May this book be the inspiration you need on those long Sundays when they have asked you to play with them 50 times before the roast potatoes have even gone into the oven.

Or give them something to do because that new series on Netflix is calling to you even louder than they are telling you that they're BORED!!!...

This is also a great collection for holidays when you have more time to devote to the smaller people (who might not find the set-up as cool, without their toys or mates, as the grown-ups do).

And there are plenty of fresh ideas here to win you parents, godparents and grandparents big points for originality when those birthday parties come around again... And again...

I hope this book will help parents in doing what all mums and dads agree to be 'the hardest job in the world'.

With apologies to crab-fishermen in the North Atlantic. It gets a bit rough out there too apparently...

QUICK
GAMES FOR
ANYWHERE

Make Your Mind Up!

Number of children needed: One–lots

Age group: 4–8 years old

Preparation and energy required from grown-up: Very little

Duration: 5–10 minutes

Equipment: None

This super-simple mind game is all about being contrary, and then trying to catch the other person out.

> One person chooses a fruit, e.g. strawberries. The other person chooses a different fruit, e.g. cherries.

> Now each person keeps saying the name of the fruit that they have chosen, fast, one after the other: 'strawberries', 'cherries', 'strawberries', 'cherries', 'strawberries'.

> After a short time or so, one person switches to the other person's fruit. So if they were

strawberries, then suddenly they defect by saying, 'Oh all right then, cherries!'

> Here's how to score points: if the other person doesn't also switch immediately to their opponent's previous choice of fruit, then they have lost a point. And if they hesitate for more than a few seconds, they have also lost a point.

(Good idea to have a fruit prize for the winner, of course.)

Free Back Massage!

> **Number of children needed:** One–lots
>
> **Age group:** 4–10 years old
>
> **Preparation and energy required from grown-up:** None
>
> **Duration:** 10 minutes
>
> **Equipment:** None

This game is based on the old favourite, Chinese Whispers, but the twist is it comes with tickling. You take it in turns to draw with your finger on the other person's back, and they guess what the object drawn is supposed to be.

Version 1

> For the first time it's best if you are the first one to draw, so they learn to do it quite slowly and make fairly big 'drawings'. Things that work are: ball (obvious, and a bit easy!), sun (add some rays), heart, star, moon, flower, tree, Christmas tree, apple, banana, rainbow, bicycle, snake, house, smiley face, sad face, ice cream with cone.

Version 2

> With older children, you can play this by writing words. They have to tickle/draw each letter of the word. Decide if the game will be done in capitals or not at the beginning, or it might get heated!

(Warning – highly addictive! It's also a great way of getting them to let you stay in bed a bit longer on a Sunday morning.)

Creep Up Behind Me

Number of children needed: Two–lots

Age group: 5–10 years old

Preparation and energy required from grown-up: First couple of times you have to be involved in the game to explain it

Duration: 10 minutes

Equipment: None

This is a classic that you probably know, but it's worth a reminder as the little 'uns love it because it's fun and competitive. Known in Spain as *Pollito Ingles* – Little English Chicken!

> Stand the children in a line outside, with you about 20 feet away from them. You face away from them and start counting.

> When you count, the children must creep towards you. They can't go too fast because every five seconds you will spin around, and they must freeze. Anyone who wobbles or giggles as you stare at them must go back to the starting place.

> It's fun to go right up to them and investigate how 'frozen' they are.

> The object of the game is for one person to reach you before you have counted to 20. The winner then becomes the one who counts and spins around – and you creep off to get some work/relaxation done.

(My daughter has figured out that giggling is her problem, so she plays the whole game with her hands over her mouth. Smart little cookie she is.)

Talking Dolls

Number of children needed: One–lots

Age group: 4–6 years old

Preparation and energy required from grown-up: 2 minutes

Duration: 10 minutes

Equipment: None

My daughter loves this game, which was inspired by her talking baby doll, and I've a feeling that we'll be playing it until she flies the nest.

> This game is perfect for when you are doing something that requires your attention, but you can also play a bit – like when you are cooking the same dish for the hundredth time or trying to get a tan...

> Choose points on the children's bodies that now become buttons which require them to say the right word or phrase when pushed.

> Start the first game with easy words and phrases, and make the next games harder. So your first game could be press the nose for 'I love you', the tummy button for 'thank you', the top of the head for 'please', the left

knee for 'let's have a cuddle' and the right knee for 'give me a kiss!'

> Now you have to test them randomly to see if they say the right phrase.

> In later games, you can have more fun with more challenging phrases, and entertain yourself in the process. 'Thank you for being the best Mummy in the world' is what my daughter has to say whenever I pull her right ear lobe.

(Obviously with more than one child, they can play this together. You can also let them turn you into a talking doll, where you have to say what they want. When my daughter presses my nose, I have to say 'Would you like some sweeties?')

Photo Fun

Number of children needed: One–lots

Age group: 4–10 years old

Preparation and energy required from grown-up: 5 minutes

Duration: 20 minutes

Equipment: Your smartphone (if you are brave enough) or a digital camera.

You will need to do the creative preparation for this game before the children take over your role – but it's a fun job for you. Your mission is to take 'half' pictures of ten different things around the house with your smartphone.

> If the children are in the house when you do this, think of a little pretend dungeon for them to hide in, with no peeking – like the utility room or the loo – until you say they can come out. Or if they are not up for pretend dungeons, then put them in a cosy bedroom and shut the door.

> So now for your photography... you could take a close-up picture of the non-brush end of a toothbrush, an aerial shot of a milk carton, Barbie's hair, a partial shot

of a slipper, a piece of cheese or broccoli, or a computer mouse.

> Take only one picture for each object, deleting any bad ones, otherwise it gets confusing.

> Now let them out of their dungeon or bedroom and give them your phone. Show them the first picture and how to scroll to find the next ones.

> Tell them they have to find all the objects and bring them to you. I usually do this with a timer, so that they can improve their speed in the next round.

> You can then tell the children that it is their turn to take ten photos of things for you to find. They love this and with a bit of luck they usually copy some of the items that you used!

> For quick-fire games or younger children, don't take partial shots of items, just take wide shots of the whole item so it is easier.

> Putting things back is of course part of the game, but they are usually so happy that this is not a problem.

(My little monkey was smart enough to photograph our rather fast-moving guinea pigs when we first played this game. How she laughed.)

Trick One – Mind-Reading Coins

Number of children needed: One–lots

Age group: 4–8 years old

Preparation or energy required from grown-up: 5 minutes

Duration: 10 minutes

Equipment: A mug or coffee cup with handle. Three coins of different value. Ideally a piece of paper and a pen, but not essential.

So you tell your young magician that you are about to teach them a magic trick that they can do anywhere, providing they have a cup or mug with a handle and three different coins. And they will always need a glamorous assistant (or you!) as this is not a solo trick.

> The secret lies in the position of the handle.

> The young magician has to learn (and so does his assistant!) that if the handle points upwards that means that there is a one pound coin underneath. Handle pointing to the right means there is a fifty pence coin. Position downwards, close to the young magician's body, means there is a twenty pence coin. Handle pointing to the left means there are no coins.

> Practise the trick a few times, so you are fully prepared to wow your guests.

> When the magic trick is mastered, you need to find your audience – preferably people with their own coins in the interests of you winning them.

> Explain that the young magician can magically tell which coin is under the cup at any time. He then turns away while the spectators watch you (lowly, but glamorous, assistant) put one of the three coins under the cup.

> Angle the handle as understood between magician and assistant, and 'hey presto', when the magician turns back around he will announce the correct coin and the audience will gasp in delight! Kerchhhing!

Make Your Own Crossword

Number of children needed: One–lots

Age group: 6–10 years old

Preparation and energy required from grown-up: 15 minutes

Duration: 20 minutes

Equipment: Pen or pencil and paper, a ruler or something similar – and definitely a rubber.

First, make a graph of a load of squares – 15 x 15 works well. You can find blank templates on the internet, but you can also make them yourself pretty fast with a pen and ruler or a book edge.

> Write simple words in the graph that overlap, crossword style. Write these very lightly in pencil, as you will need to rub them out before you hand over the masterpiece.

> Then black out the spaces that you don't need. It doesn't matter if there are quite a few.

> Then number the words. Go from the top left corner, and number them moving to the right. Keep the numbers moving in that direction only, as you would read a piece of text, making a note of whether the clues are down or

across, and be strict about this, otherwise you will get into a mess.

> Now write clues that are funny for the whole family, e.g. if Cousin Emily hates bananas, write a clue such as 'Emily's favourite yellow food'. Or if Dad is always late home from work, 'What time does Dad usually get home from work?' – answer might be 'late'.

(Educationally, this was great for teaching my daughter the meaning of 'the opposite of' and 'sounds like', i.e. 'This is the opposite of fast, like Sarah doing her homework' where the answer would be 'slow', or 'It sounds like wagon, but it has four legs not four wheels, and blows fire out of its mouth' would be 'dragon'.)

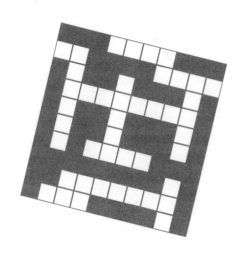

Speedy Wordsearch

Number of children needed: One–lots

Age group: 7–10 years old

Preparation and energy required from grown-up: 15 minutes

Duration: 20 minutes

Equipment: Pen or pencil, paper, a ruler (or something similar) and a timer.

This is the DIY version of the mind-bogglingly brilliant game, Boggle – should you have foolishly left home without it, or lost it – or even worse, never bought it!

> For those who haven't come across it before, Boggle is a plastic cube containing 16 dice with letters of the alphabet on them. You shake the box and allow the letters to settle at random into the grid. An egg timer is turned over and each player must find and write down as many words as they can find in the pattern of letters. The letters must adjoin in a chain which can be read horizontally, vertically or diagonally. The person with the most words wins.

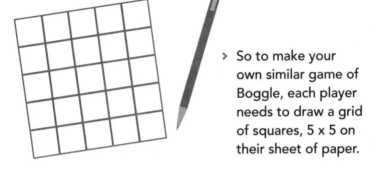

> So to make your own similar game of Boggle, each player needs to draw a grid of squares, 5 x 5 on their sheet of paper.

> Then each player in turn says a letter, while the adult writes that letter in a box in the grid, at random. Keep going until all 25 boxes have been filled. Each letter needs to be called out no more than two seconds after the last one, to keep the game moving fast and stop any clever clogs from actually writing fully formed words at this stage.

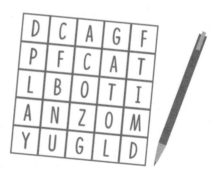

> The same letter cannot be called out more than three times.

> When the grid has been filled, the game is ready to play. Set a time limit of three minutes and now everyone must start to write down words (over two letters long) that they can see in their grid – horizontally, vertically or diagonally.

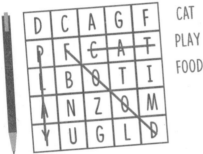

CAT

PLAY

FOOD

> When the time is up, score yourselves and check your competitors for any cheating! A point per letter in each word, and a bonus point for any smarty-pants that managed to find a five-letter word!

★ **Turn Them Into Magicians** ★

Trick Two – Double Your Money!

Number of children needed: One–lots

Age group: 7–10 years old

Preparation and energy required from grown-up: 15 minutes

Duration: 20 minutes

Equipment: Six coins and a glossy magazine.

This trick may inspire your little dream-home-in-the-sun funders to pursue lucrative careers in banking OR become the next Dynamo. In the case of the latter then they will have a lot more celebrity friends. There's always a downside to every plan...

> You can either do this trick on the children, and then teach them how to do it, or learn the trick together.

> In advance of the performance, a magazine is placed where the magic trick will be done. Three secret coins are placed inside the magazine, on different pages.

> When the time comes to do the trick, this magazine will be selected – as if a glossy surface is needed for the trick. This is a ruse, of course. It is a good idea for the young magician to fake looking around for other glossy surfaces, i.e. pretend to check out the glossiness of adjacent magazines, or the table, and then decide on the one with the secret stash within.

> Now the young magician must ask an audience member whether they have three coins, and if they would like to turn them into six coins.

> When the audience member says 'yes' (or 'stupid question!') they should be asked to place their coins on top of the magazine.

> The magician must carefully fold the magazine and let the coins slide into their hand. All six will fall into the magician's hand, but the magician must make a fist so no one can see the loot at this stage.

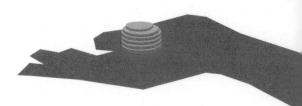

> Now the magician must hop or dance dramatically around saying abracadabra to their fist, taking the emphasis away from that magazine!

> Then for the big reveal of the six coins in their hand!

(The magician may now cheekily declare the booty as payment for the trick!)

GAMES FOR
INDOORS

20 Questions

Number of children needed: One–lots

Age group: 5–10 years old

Preparation or energy required from grown-up: Very little

Duration: 20 minutes

Equipment: Paper and pencils or pens, sticky tape.

Version 1

Tell each contender they have to think of something or someone to be.

This could be:

- an object in the room that you are in

- something to eat

- a children's TV or movie character

- a teacher or friend that everyone in the family knows.

> Tell children that now, to find out what or who the other person is, each player has to ask questions but the only answer the other player can give is 'Yes' or 'No'.

> The first person to guess who or what the other person is wins.

Version 2

A more fun version of this game requires a little bit more effort from you. The kids not only need to come up with someone or something, but also need to draw it on a piece of paper. The one that has to guess is not allowed to see it (banished under the table or under a towel) and will have this someone or something taped onto their back. Children then take turns guessing in the same way as above – 'Yes' or 'No' answers only.

NB: Tell them that they have to decide on one category for each round, i.e. animals/things/food – otherwise it's too difficult.

For older ones, you can suggest questions with more specific answers, such as for the animal category:

▪ What colour am I?

▪ Do I make a lot of noise? (not allowed to do the noise though – too easy)

- How many legs have I got?

- Do I like hot or cold countries?

- Am I big or small?

- What do I eat?

- Can I fly?

- Can I swim?

(If the team can read then it's a good idea to write the clue questions on a piece of paper. Then they can play more easily on their own, while you get to read the actual paper...)

Fetch!

Number of children needed: One–lots

Age group: 3–6 years old

Preparation or energy required from grown-up: 5 minutes for explaining the rules

Duration: 15–20 minutes

Equipment: Things in the house.

Tell your children that today they are cute little puppies and their job is to fetch things.

> First they have to find something coloured white from the bathroom (if it hasn't run out again…). The first one to come back with something gets a point.

> Next, they must find something soft from a bedroom.

> Next, they have to find something that belongs to Mummy that is pink.

> Next, something green that doesn't smell of anything.

> Next, something that Daddy hasn't used for a long time.

> Next, a piece of clothing that has the colour blue in it.

> Next, something that has somebody's name written on it.

> Next, something that smells nice.

> Give them the scores, and then make them have a race to put the stuff they found back in its rightful place – very important!

> If you have multiple offspring or a party on your hands, and the children are old enough to read, you can give them a different list of five things each and make it a race.

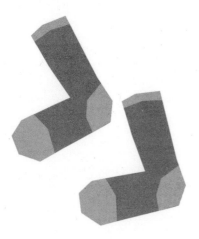

Mime It For Me

Number of children needed: Two–lots

Age group: 4–8 years old

Preparation or energy required from grown-up: 10 minutes

Duration: 25 minutes

Equipment: Paper and pen, box to put bits of paper in – or (if you want to be flash) a hat – a stopwatch on your phone or an egg timer.

Tell the children that today you are a big-shot movie director and you need to see their acting skills to see if you can make them rich and famous.

> This is the perfect game for nurturing thespians or – let's think more positively – major Hollywood movie stars (and a good game should any naughty grown-ups have a bit of a hangover on a Saturday morning as the children have to be nice and quiet!).

> Create a stage area, and split the children into two teams – or one against one will still work. Flip a coin to see which team starts first.

> Write things for the children to 'act out' on pieces of paper and put them in the box (or hat). The first team starts and pulls out a piece of paper containing something they must act out, while you operate the timer. They must mime the action to the other child if there are only two players, or to the members of their own team if you have bigger teams. The object of the game is to be good at miming the action to enable the others to guess it – so points are given for the acting, NOT the guessing.

> If you give them a minute and a half they should be able to 'act out' two or three of the actions that they pick out. (If not, maybe think about tennis lessons because perhaps they are not headed for Hollywood after all.)

> Shout 'action' and 'cut' at the beginning and end of time. (Go on, treat yourself...)

> Make sure they don't throw the 'used' actions back into the box or hat. Ideally you should be grabbing each 'guessed' bit of paper and thus doing the scoring.

NB: for younger children who can't read, you'll need to whisper each action to them. Useful to play near a door you can hide behind for whispering – or have a towel to whisper underneath while the other kids have to sing so they can't hear.

Suggestions for actions:

- getting dressed
- making a cup of tea
- riding a motorbike
- taking photos
- changing a baby's nappy
- taking a dog for a walk
- cleaning teeth
- talking on the phone
- swimming fast to avoid jellyfish!
- ironing
- swimming slowly
- singing
- washing hair
- dancing, working on a computer
- flipping pancakes
- driving a car

Mime It For Me (Professions)

Number of children needed: Two–lots

Age group: 4–12 years old

Preparation and energy required from grown-up: It's a sit-down job for you, but hands-on

Duration: 25 minutes

Equipment: Paper and pen, box to put bits of paper in – or (if you want to be flash) a hat – a stopwatch on your phone or an egg timer.

This is the same concept as Mime It For Me, as above, but with professions. It's less fast-paced as it is more difficult, so be generous and give each team four minutes per round. They are not allowed to speak, but you should let them do soundtrack noise where necessary.

> Unless your children are total geniuses, you will probably need to whisper little ideas to help them with this game, or put them into pairs, or you might have to join in a bit – i.e. you pay the taxi driver, or you are the customer for the hairdresser, or you get on the bus and pay the driver.

Suggestions for professions:

- teacher
- singer, postman
- aeroplane pilot
- dancer
- chef
- waitress
- dentist

- doctor
- taxi driver
- hairdresser
- bus driver
- supermodel
- racing driver.

Trick Three – Making Pepper Swim

> **Number of children needed:** One–lots
>
> **Age group:** 6–10 years old
>
> **Preparation or energy required from grown-up:** 5 minutes
>
> **Duration:** 10 minutes
>
> **Equipment:** A shallow bowl, milk, black pepper, washing-up liquid, an espresso coffee cup or a freezer bag, jacket for the magician or sweatshirt with big pocket.

This trick is quite impressive as nobody guesses the secret if it's performed well.

> It is a solo trick, so when you have taught children this you will enjoy watching them impress friends and family.

> In preparation for the magic, a tiny amount of washing-up liquid is required to be deposited in either an espresso coffee cup or within a freezer bag in the young magician's right-hand pocket of their jacket.

> Put some milk into a shallow bowl. Shake some pepper on top and tell the audience that pepper can be made to swim with a little magic!

> Now a little abracadabra-ness is required – flamboyantly, of course – from the young magician.

> While this is occurring, they must put their index finger surreptitiously into the tiny little cup or freezer bag in their pocket containing the washing-up liquid.

> This magic finger must then dabble in the milk.

> The pepper will swim… and jaws will drop!

What Am I Drawing?

Number of children needed: Two–lots

Age group: 6–12 years old

Preparation or energy required from grown-up: 5 minutes. Mainly whispering to little ones.

Duration: 20–25 minutes

Equipment: Paper and pen, box to put bits of paper in, a stopwatch on your phone or an egg timer, and either a blackboard and chalk or plenty of sheets of A4 paper that you can tape to a door or wall. Ideally, sticky tape or sticky tack.

Obviously no prizes for originality in this game (it bears a resemblance to Pictionary) – but maybe you grew up in a cave and never got to play.

> Write down objects on bits of paper and put them in a box/hat.

> Split the children into two teams – again, if you only have two children, playing against each other will still work.

> The points are given for good drawing, therefore enabling correct guessing. Points are NOT given for guessing.

> The oldest child goes first – they can usually draw better – and anyway the youngest child always gets to go first in board games.

> They must draw the first object written on the piece of paper they pull out of the box. Again, if they are young you will have to read it for them and whisper to them.

> Time them – three minutes per round is about right. Hopefully they will have time to draw more than one object and have it guessed correctly.

> Children younger than six do like this game but, in my experience, can only really draw flowers, hearts and weird looking cats. Depends on the tolerance/niceness of the older children playing with them...

Suggestions for objects:

- cat
- tree
- shark
- banana
- shoe
- ice cream
- boat
- car
- suitcase
- aeroplane
- scissors
- tennis racquet
- apple
- bicycle
- T-shirt
- dress
- television
- chair
- table
- moon
- fish
- bed
- umbrella
- hat
- sunglasses
- box
- frying pan.

★ **Turn Them Into Magicians** ★

Trick Four –
The Bag Magic Trick
(Mind Reading By Colours)

Number of children needed: Two–lots

Age group: 6–10 years old

Preparation and energy required from grown-up: 5 minutes to explain

Duration: 15 minutes

Equipment: Handbag (with contents).

You will need two magicians and an audience – so child and parent with audience or two kids performing magic for the audience.

> In this trick, the magician and their assistant will magically mind-read a member of the audience who is thinking of a randomly chosen object from the contents of a handbag.

> First the magicians must read and understand the clever key to the trick. (Look away now, grown-up, if you want to hand the book to an older child and get a nice surprise.)

> The key to the trick is that the assistant mentions the colour of the object they say before they say the object chosen, i.e. Is it the make-up bag? No. Is it the keys? No. Is it the bottle of water? No. Is it the pink hairbrush? No. Is it the diary? YES!

> So a member of the audience is asked to whisper an object to the assistant, while the magician is sent out of the room. When the magician returns, the assistant asks the questions.

> Cue amazement from all the family...

What's In The Bag/ Box Now?

Number of children needed: Two–lots

Age group: 4–10 years old

Preparation and energy required from grown-up: 10–15 minutes

Duration: 15 minutes

Equipment: A box or rucksack about twice the size of a shoe box. Scissors to cut hole in box if you have a box. Something for a blindfold, e.g. a scarf. NB: Travel blindfolds are very cheap and a good investment for many games! Selection of objects from home and the toy box. Nothing sharp.

The idea of the game is that the child whose turn it is gets blindfolded, and then puts one hand in the box and finds an object which they must identify just by feeling it. They are not allowed to pull it out and reveal what it is until they have guessed it correctly. This needs a bit of policing, as if they pull the object out before they have guessed what it is, it tends to be a bit of a spoiler for the others.

> Also in need of monitoring is the tendency from the youngsters to pretend that the blindfold is on properly when it's not. I like to do random testing now and then, by asking them how many fingers I am holding up, while holding a surprise object in front of them like a pair of tweezers. You can just tell by the allegedly blindfolded child's reactions to this question whether they are destined for a life of crime or not! On top of which it amuses the others.

> Place all the objects in the box or bag, and sit the kids around a table.

> Blindfold the first child. Ask them to dip their hand nice and slowly into the box or bag and grab hold of something. It's fun to whisper 'Mind the spiders!' at this point.

> If a player can't guess the object that they have selected after 90 seconds then they have to give up and it's the next person's turn.

Suggestions for objects
(nothing with sharp edges) are:

- toothbrush
- egg (hard boiled obviously)
- apple
- banana
- old mobile phone
- pen
- clothes peg
- spoon
- small toys such as toy cars
- plastic animals (but they have to identify the animal not just announce that it is a plastic animal)
- Dad's smelly sock of course
- dolly (always very amusing for the others when a boy pulls that one out – especially if Barbie is naked, as she tends to be in our house even though she has more dresses than Mummy).

What's In The Bag/Box Now? –
Round Two, What's Missing?

> If it's still raining or dinner is ages away, put eight objects on the table and hold the box/bag close to your chest.

> The little geniuses must study all the objects on the table. Repeat the names of the objects together. (If the children are learning a language, do this in that language if possible.)

> Now tell them to go under the table and shut their eyes, while you deftly remove an object and put it in the box/bag.

> Then up they come and the first person to work out which object is missing wins a point.

> Continue the game by removing another object, and so on. You can also move two or three objects at a time to keep them on their toes. Or let them take over from you as the hider of the objects, while you plate up – or pour a glass of wine!

Hot Seat

Number of children needed: One–lots

Age group: 4–12 years old

Preparation or energy required from grown-up: 5 minutes

Duration: 15 minutes

Equipment: Approx. 20 sheets of A4 paper, tape and felt-tip pens.

Sit down Hot Seat Kid *Numero Uno* with their back to a big sheet of paper stuck up on the door or wall behind them.

> Tell them 'NO PEEKING'. And be aware of mirrors – the cheating types will never confess that they have seen the answers through the sly use of a mirror.

> As games master here, you need to draw an object on the paper. (If playing with older children who are good at drawing then they can take up this role.) Suggested objects are a banana, a tree, a bicycle, a sailing boat, a car, a princess, a rocket, a cat, an ice cream, a bar of chocolate or an umbrella.

> Now tell the remaining little ones, who are facing the drawing, to describe the object to the Hot Seat Kid by giving them clues as to what it is. For example:

  - Banana – it's a fruit, it's yellow, you peel it to eat it…

  - Tree – it's normally very big, you see lots of them in parks, they are green…

  - Bicycle – it has two wheels, you have to learn to ride it, mine is pink…

> Score the game. You award points for the descriptions, not the guesses – that's the easier bit…

> Whoever gives the last clue that clinches it for the Hot Seat Kid becomes the Hot Seat Kid next.

Sweet-Bobbing (Or A Naughty Version Of Apple Bobbing)

Number of children needed: One–lots

Age group: 7–10 years old

Preparation and energy required from grown-up: 10 minutes

Duration: 15–20 minutes

Equipment: Wrapped sweets, bowl of water.

This is a Halloween classic that deserves to be played more than once a year. And if you switch apples for sweets then the kids will love you to Pluto and back (but might be slightly disappointed at Halloween parties...).

> Put six sweeties (don't make it too easy for them) in a big plastic bowl – a washing-up bowl works – and fill it up with water.

> Sit the tribe on the floor around the bowl of water, with some towels underneath it to soak up splashes. Now ask them one at a time to put their hands behind

their backs and get hold of the sweeties without using their hands. Give them strict time limits with an egg timer or your phone (from a safe distance to avoid getting splashed...).

Trick Five – Making The Ketchup Move

Number of children needed: One–lots

Age group: 6–10 years old

Preparation and energy required from grown-up: 5 minutes

Duration: 10 minutes

Equipment: A 1.5-litre (or similar) plastic water or drinks bottle. A sachet of ketchup.

A great little trick in which it looks like your budding illusionists can make a sachet of ketchup move up and down inside a bottle by using the power of their brilliant young minds.

> Put the sachet in the water bottle and fill the bottle with water.

> With one hand, they should theatrically ask the sachet to move up or down – and verbally too of course.

> With the other hand holding the bottle they surreptitiously squeeze the bottle.

> It's magic. But practice makes perfect.

Pin The Tail On The Donkey (And Other Animals!)

Number of children needed: One–lots

Age group: 4–9 years old

Preparation and energy required from grown-up: 5 minutes

Duration: 15 minutes

Equipment: Blackboard and chalk – or whiteboard and pens – or large sheets of paper and sticky tape or sticky tack.

The classic birthday party games such as musical statues, musical chairs and pass the parcel are great of course, but everybody's favourite does seem to be the blindfolded, dizzy morning after fun of Pin the Tail on the Donkey.

> You can do this with a blackboard or by just sticking a few A4 pieces of paper together and taping them to the wall, then drawing the outline of a tail-less animal in thick pen. It doesn't have to be a donkey… it could be a pig, a cow, an elephant, a cat, a dog.

> Create a tail out of paper and add a bit of folded sticky tape (or sticky tack) on its thicker end.

> Now decide on the order of play by tapping each kid on the head with a number, starting from one. Explain that they will all have their turn.

> Blindfold kid number one and put said tail in their hand. Tell them to pin the tail on the donkey!

> Spin them around while everyone counts to ten (note some kids can only manage five spins.

> Cue giggles galore as they dizzily miss their mark!

> It's very easy to spot the cheats as they get it spot on! They don't even aim convincingly quite close...

(TIP – Encourage the players to feel their surroundings before the blindfold goes on.)

Octopus Friends (A Craft Idea)

Number of children needed: One–lots

Age group: 3–8 years old

Preparation and energy required from grown-up: 5 minutes. Do one, for an example, and let the others continue your good work.

Duration: 15–20 minutes

Equipment: Two loo roll inner tubes per kid, plus kids' scissors, crayons, glue and pieces of paper. Optional yoghurt pots. For the deluxe version you need bubble wrap and a ping-pong ball and paint or felt-tips.

You are making a little octopus and helping your child count to eight. What could be more fun?

> Let them cut into the loo roll tube from one end with scissors until nearly halfway up. They must do this eight times to create the arms of the octopus.

> Next, take each of the eight cut strips of the tube and curl the 'arms' of this little fellow so that he can stand up and be counted – and made gorgeous.

> The little artists must now crayon some lovely big eyes, a pouty mouth and maybe lots of clashing colours in small stripes on his lovely arms, so that this little friend can frighten his enemies in the sea.

> If you have any empty yoghurt pots that you have had the inclination to wash-up they can make a very nice addition as the head – otherwise the head needs to be made of the second loo roll pushed into a bit of a bump shape and taped on.

For the lucky deluxe octopus with a bubble-wrapped head

For clever people who saved the bubble wrap at Christmas AND know where they put it, you will need to cut out an A4–sized piece of bubble wrap.

> Place a ping-pong ball in the centre of the bubble wrap and wrap the bubble wrap around the ball, securing it with a rubber band or a piece of string.

> Then make eight cuts into the 'skirt'. Now roll up the legs and tape them together at the ends, to create a tapered effect. The bubble wrap gives a great tentacle effect. Now leave your child to decorate the octopus with paint or felt-tips, showing them where to draw the eyes and a mouth.

> Then you might explain that octopi are very clever creatures who build their own beautiful gardens of shells and stones on the sea floor... cue garden treasure hunting!

> These beauties can be suspended with string from window frames or ceilings for admiration purposes and their search of course for their own octopus gardens...

Chopstick Marbles

Number of children needed: One–lots

Age group: 6–10 years old

Preparation and energy required from grown-up: Procuring the equipment listed below

Duration: 10 minutes

Equipment: A set of chopsticks per player (same size), marbles (ideally different sizes) and preferably ping-pong balls and tennis balls too. Two plastic containers.

This amusing little number can be played as a race if there are a few of you, or just as a little bit of fun before dinner if you are a smaller-sized gang.

> If your marbles are all the same size you can still play this but ideally you would have a selection of different sizes. If under-sevens are involved you'll also need ping-pong balls, which are easier to capture so the younger ones don't get too frustrated.

> Start by placing all the balls in one container and place the other (empty) container about a metre away.

> Give all the players a pair of chopsticks each and teach them how to hold them – low down gives more control, closer to the thinner ends that grown-ups use to pick up their noodles.

> Explain that on the count of three, players must use their chopsticks to pick up a ball from the full container and deliver it to the empty container... the person who delivers the most balls in five minutes wins.

> If balls are dropped on the floor, then chopsticks must be used to pick them up again. Failing that, then one hand only must be used to place the ball back on the chopsticks.

(NB: if the chopsticks get too frustrating for little ones, then just use soup spoons.)

Pass The Salt, Will You?

Number of children needed: Six–lots

Age group: 4–6 years old

Preparation and energy required from grown-up: None

Duration: 10 minutes

Equipment: Objects to pass around: a salt pot (if you can close it), or oranges or tangerines. And some feet in clean-ish socks!

Time for lots of rolling around on the floor for this game – so ideally play it in a room with a carpet to avoid bumped heads.

> Line up two teams.

> Each team has to use one hand only to pass an object between them. The object must be something small that a little hand can hold comfortably, such as a tangerine, and must be passed to the person sitting next to them.

> On the way up the line only the right hand can be used, and only the left hand can be used on the way down. If they are still

learning left and right, draw the letters L and R on the appropriate hands. They should have it cracked after a few games of this!

> Next they play the game passing the object to each other only using their feet. Strictly no hands!

> Cue lots of giggles and consternation depending on ages. This is a great way to kill ten minutes.

Princes And Princesses

Number of children needed: Two–lots

Age group: 4–9 years old

Preparation and energy required from grown-up: None

Duration: 20 minutes

Equipment: One cushion per child and some music to play.

This is an embellished version of musical statues which is amusing for adults to watch, and for which the adults get to pretend to be royalty. (If you don't already on a daily basis...)

> Every player needs to be given a cushion – one not too much bigger than their head!

> Next tell your subjects or courtiers that you are the Queen or King and that today there is dancing in your court. Not only dancing, but dancing with a cushion on their hand. But when the music stops each subject must go down on

one knee and say 'Greetings, Your Majesty', without losing their cushion, and then get up again when the music re-starts.

> Anyone who lets their cushion slide off their head – well apologies but it is simply off with their heads! Eliminated!

> In the event of there not being equally sized cushions to hand out then follow-up rounds will need to be played to make things equal. All is fair in court!

Smelly Shoe And Sock Detectives

Number of children needed: Six children and adults (minimum)

Age group: 4–10 years old

Preparation and energy required from grown-up: None

Duration: 10 minutes

Equipment: Shoes, socks and a blindfold – a travel blindfold is worth investing in for games. These can be purchased in pound shops or inexpensively online and save you struggling with slippery scarves which make it easier for kids to cheat.

This is a very simple game but 'a bit of a hoot', as my mother used to say.

> So to kick off, everybody has to kick off their smelly shoes and socks and put them in a pile. Muddle them all up – shuffle those socks and shoes!

> Now the first person to play puts on the blindfold and grapples around in the pile to try to find their own shoes and socks and also to put them on. Encourage lots of sniffing as well as grappling about.

> Very important that everybody stifles the giggles if the player puts on the wrong socks or shoes – until the blindfold is off. When the cat is out of the bag, as it were, then of course everyone can cackle away!

> Before the next player has a go, all the shoes and socks must be back in the pile. The sock and shoe stack must be muddled up again when the blindfold is on the next player.

Flying Fish

Number of children needed: One–lots

Age group: 4–10 years old

Preparation and energy required from grown-up: None

Duration: 15 minutes

Equipment: Paper, A4 thin card, scissors, pens or crayons, newspaper to roll up for each player.

This little section is a reminder that all children love being the masters of things that fly. Hopefully not always including your best wine glasses...

> So each player needs a piece of thin card to make a beautiful fish out of, about twice the size of a grown-up hand. Their fish must be beautifully decorated with their finest felt-tips and cut out – accurately-ish.

> The fish now need to be helped to swim, flutter and fly down a long hallway or across a big room (carpet doesn't work that well though). No touching of the fish is allowed – the transportation device is a tightly rolled up newspaper or magazine that must be blown through to help the fish scoot along to the end of the race. The

players will need to get down on their tummies and wriggle like eels as they blow.

> Drinking straws can also be used if the fish paper is very lightweight.

> May the best fishy winny!

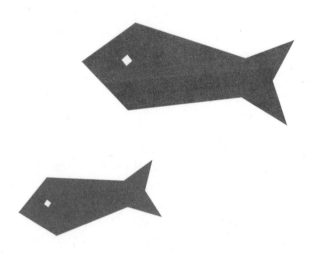

Drawing Stories In The Dark

Number of children needed: Two–lots

Age group: 7–12 years old

Preparation and energy required from grown-up: A little creativity to tell a silly story

Duration: 20 minutes

Equipment: Paper and pens, a table to all sit at together, and a room that will go properly scarily dark when the lights are out. If not, blindfolds at the ready!

First, clear some space on the fridge to put these comedy masterpieces on when you have finished! Time to throw out that Father Christmas painting that looks just a little bit like mashed potato and ketchup... maybe it is!

> Sit the children at the table with an A4 piece of paper each, landscape format. And ideally one fairly fat felt-tip pen each – if not, any old pen will work.

> Tell them they are going to draw a few pictures on this paper, illustrating your lovely story that they are about to hear. Tell them to start top left, and work to the right. There will be about ten pictures to draw, so tell them to keep their drawings quite small.

> Now turn out all the lights so it is completely dark – or blindfold them with travel blindfolds or scarves.

> Now start your story. Each time you want them to draw something from the story, emphasise the word and pause for about one minute to give them time to scribble their artist-in-the-dark impressions.

> Don't stress about your story making much sense or having a moral to it. This is just for fun. I end mine every time with 'and then they all went to BED' no matter what has gone on beforehand!

> With older kids especially, it is fun to have a scary story and make them draw ghosts, witches, clown faces, zombies, a monster having his head chopped off with an axe, etc. Throw some normal things into the story like a bunch of flowers, a bicycle, a cup of tea, an umbrella, as the juxtaposition is very funny.

> With younger ones, your story needs to involve things that they think they can draw when not in the dark or blindfolded. So keep it simple. Turn the lights on and compare the drawings! Lots of laughs.

Story suggestion:

One day an APPLE went for a walk and found his friend the BANANA crying under a TREE. 'What's the matter?' asked the apple. 'I have lost my MOBILE PHONE,' said the banana. 'Oh dear,' said the apple, 'where did you see it last?' 'In my HOUSE,' said the banana. 'Ah,' said the apple, 'Well let's go to your house. It must still be there.' To cheer the banana up, the apple bought him an ICE CREAM on the way. When they got to the banana's house, they could hear a noise coming from the FRIDGE. They opened the fridge and the phone was inside! The banana's mum was on the phone, to say she had made a nice BIRTHDAY CAKE for the banana's birthday next week. They had a nice CUP OF TEA and talked about really cool birthday games that you can play with a BALLOON. Then they were so tired they went to BED.

Surprise!!! Stories

Number of children needed: One–lots

Age group: 7–10 years old

Preparation and energy required from grown-up: 2 minutes to explain

Duration: 10 minutes

Equipment: Paper, pens or pencils.

This is a great little time-killer and will put the grumpiest of grizzlers in a good mood if you steer it well.

> Begin by writing the opening sentence of a story (which is completely undiscussed in advance) without anyone else seeing what you have written. Leave the sentence without a full stop so the story can continue, and with an 'and' or a 'but' or a 'and then'.

> The paper is now folded, backwards (away from you) so that the words are concealed, and the paper is passed to the next aspiring author. They continue the story with a new sentence ending in 'and' or 'but', ready for the next person to continue the story.

> Keep going between you, always being top, top, top secretive...

> When the page is fully used up (an A4 sheet should give you room for about ten sentences) it's time for the big reveal...

> The grown-up gets to read and little ones get to giggle at the silliest story ever.

(To maximise the humour it is funnier if the grown-up writes in quite a grown-up way, juxtaposed with princesses kissing frogs, monsters flying into castles and people doing windy-pops.)

Slap Jack

Number of children needed: Two–five

Age group: 4–8 years old

Preparation and energy required from grown-up: Hardly any

Duration: 5–10 minutes

Equipment: Deck of playing cards.

Little ones feel very grown up playing this game because...

1. It is using the cards that grown-ups play with but it is easy peasy.

2. The only cards that they have to understand or recognise are those princely Jacks.

3. They get to do a lot of boisterous slapping of their hands without getting told off!

> The grown-up must deal the cards equally.

> Each player tidies up their pile of cards and puts them face down in front of them.

> In the middle of you all, or the centre of the table, the grown-up now declares as the playing area.

> Time for the festivity to commence.

> The first person to play (whoever did the washing-up or homework without grumbling) places the first card from their pile, face up, in the playing area.

> The next person places theirs, etc. LOOK OUT FOR JACKS!

> When anyone places a Jack, this necessitates a speedy manoeuvre to slam one's hand on top of the pile in the middle, and shout 'GOT YOU, JACK!'

> Whoever gets there first wins the whole pile!

> And so on, and so on.

> The object of the game is to win all the cards.

Rule 1

Anyone who gets slap-happy, i.e. slams their hand on any card other than a Jack, has to forfeit a card from their pile to each of their competitors.

Rule 2 (but it's a nice one)

Anyone who loses all their pile is not out. They can still observe and play... and let's hope their grubby little mitts move fast!

Speed

Number of children needed: Two

Age group: 7–10 years old

Preparation and energy required from grown-up: 3 minutes

Duration: 5–10 minutes

Equipment: Deck of cards.

This is my favourite card game ever and I played it endlessly with my sister from I think around the age of eight until I was at least 15. We were more addicted to this than choccy biscuits.

> To set up the game, each player must face each other over a coffee table or similar. Proximity and being opposite each other is vital.

> You need five piles of cards in front of each player, but the piles must vary in size. Do this by splitting the pack in two and handing half to each player.

> Now start creating each person's set-up.

> First lay one card face up, and to the right of that card place four cards face down in a nice row heading to the right.

> Next go back to the left of the arrangement, and place a card face up on top of the second card.

> Continue to place others face down on top of the rest of the cards to the right.

> Now continue. Place a card face up on the third card, and face down on the fourth and fifth.

> Continue until the fifth pile has a card face up on the top, and four cards facing down underneath.

> In fact, before the 'racey' game commences, each player now gets a chance to organise their cards in a way that might maximise their speed and skill...

> If any player has two of the same number displayed, they are allowed to put the said matching cards together, as if they were brother and sister, and then reveal the cards that were underneath!

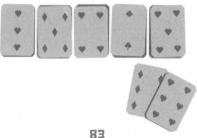

> The aim of the game is to get your hands on as many different number cards that are visible to you as possible.

> Now it is time to play.

> Each player puts their leftover pile of cards face-down to the right of their five small piles of cards.

> On the count of three, each player turns over a card, and places it face-up to the left of their pile of cards. So two races begin at the same time. But the fun bit is that each player must exploit both stacks of cards to win!

> Now it is a fast race basically to slam any card one under or over in numerical value on top of either of those cards in both piles.

> As the game continues, and you quickly slam your cards down on either pile, you can uncover any cards you had behind the front-facing ones. Five cards can be viewed at any one time!

› Strategy comes into play when you can observe your opponents' cards. For example, if one player can see that they have cards that would work well upwards of seven (i.e. eight, nine, ten, Jack) but that their opponent has cards of lower numbers, then they might hesitate to put down a six.

(For smaller kids, laying out the cards at the beginning of the game is the issue. But teach them, adults, and they will play this with siblings or friends for years because it is all about that important buzz to children – speed!)

GAMES FOR THE GARDEN

Darts For All

Number of children needed: Two–lots

Age group: 4–10 years old

Preparation and energy required from grown-up: 15 minutes preparation and very little energy, but you will need to adjudicate/prevent war

Duration: 20 minutes

Equipment: A3 card, felt-tip pens, duct tape and (if playing with older kids) small stones or pebbles as they travel well when thrown. If playing with kids under five you will need plastic bottle tops.

Basically, you need to create a kind of giant dartboard. You draw ten big circles on the A3 card – they should be different sizes, with the smallest in the middle, and the circles should fill the card. Then write the numbers 1 – 10 at the top of each circle (10 should be in the middle).

> Then draw objects underneath each number. For comedic purposes, draw objects that the children like more as the numbers increase:

1. Broccoli – come on, it's only like drawing small trees – if you can't then draw peas...

2. An alarm clock

3. A bed

4. A ball

5. A kitten – it's only like drawing a small cat

6. A puppy – TIP: it's all in the floppy ears

7. An ice cream

8. A car

9. A speed boat or sailing boat

10. A holiday – beach, brolly, bucket and spade. If that's too hard, draw a rocket flying to the moon.

> Fix your dartboard with tape onto the ground. Ideally you should do this near a raised step which smaller children can stand on to help with their little trajectories.

> Let the games commence. Each player takes it in turn to fire darts or throw stones onto the high numbers. Score

for them, or if you have stuff to do then make them score each other.

> Play ten rounds, or until you're tired!

> I play this to teach English to children, so they must say the name of the object to win a point. If your children are learning a language you could apply the same rule.

Pick-Up Sticks

Number of children needed: Two–lots

Age group: 4–10 years old

Preparation and energy required from grown-up: None

Duration: 20 minutes

Equipment: Sticks – twigs and, if available, bigger twigs. But they should all be very light and manageable.

Mikado is the Japanese name for this but it's just known as *Pick-Up Sticks* in our house.

> Send the kids into the garden to find little sticks and twigs. They shouldn't be any bigger than a drinking straw, although the odd big one works well.

> Then they have to strip off any mini-branches or off-shoots from their collection. To do this they can just rub the sticks together, hopefully without anyone catching on fire…

> When you have approved of the smoothed twig collection, then collect them in one pile and stack them up on a smooth, level surface – like making a fire.

> Now the game can begin and each player in turn has to remove a stick without moving the others.

> If any judders or tremors are detected in the pile, it's the next person's go.

> If anyone removes a stick without judders or tremors, then they get another go.

> The kid with the most sticks at the end wins.

(This game can be played indoors of course, or in a bar or restaurant when your kids are bored if you can get hold of a pile of drinking straws and a separate table for them to play where nothing can be broken...)

Duck, Duck, Goose

Number of children needed: Four–lots

Age group: 4–10 years old

Preparation and energy required from grown-up: None

Duration: 10 minutes

Equipment: None

Kids love this game for three reasons:

1. They get to be in charge (when it's their turn to be the goose) and fuel the action, so they are the absolute centre of attention.

2. They have the exciting anticipation (when they are ducks) of wondering if they will be 'chosen'.

3. They get to run around in circles. (Great training for adulthood...)

> Sit them in a circle and join them for the first round or three to show them how it's done.

> Explain that in each round of the game, one person is a goose and the others are ducks.

> Now explain that you, being the goose, will walk (quite slowly, building suspense) around the circle and tap everyone on the head. When a player hears the word 'DUCK' as they are tapped on the head, then they stay sitting down. When a player hears the word 'GOOSE' as they are tapped on the head, then they must jump up and run after the GOOSE (around the circle of players) to try to tag the goose, i.e. catch up with the goose BEFORE it sits down in the space just vacated.

> If the goose-that-just-chose-a-new-goose makes it to the newly vacated place before the newly tapped goose tags them, then the old goose is now a duck, and the not-fast-enough-duck is now the goose, ready to do the tapping.

> Quacking stuff.

(Particularly attention-seeking kids will walk round the circle tapping heads for way more than one circuit, soaking up the glory of being the boss. Policing required! Generally, it all works out because the less 'me-me-me' children are tolerant of those that like to hog the limelight!)

London

> **Number of children needed:** One–lots
>
> **Age group:** 4–10 years old
>
> **Preparation and energy required from grown-up:** None
>
> **Duration:** 20 minutes
>
> **Equipment:** Chalk (different colours if you have them) and a small toy or stone.

Scrabbling around on the ground outside with chalk and a purpose is most kids' equivalent to a good bottle of wine and a great movie. They will love you for this one.

> To play this classic British game you need a good-sized patch of (preferably smooth) tarmac, unless you have very fat chalk or plenty of ordinary chalk as it will snap a lot! A patio surface that chalk shows up on well will also work.

> To start with the grown-up will need to draw a skyscraper on the ground with chalk. Around seven floors will do it, with each rectangular floor being about the size of a tea towel. At the top of the skyscraper make a nice roof and inside the roof write the word LONDON. (With

older children – over eight – the floors can be thinner and narrower to be more challenging, but keep them tea towel-sized for younger ones.)

> Now gather the troops (or child) and explain the rules and the object of the game.

> The winner will be the first person to finish drawing three stick men working in their offices in the skyscraper – but rather like hangman, a player can only draw the stick men in stages: head first, then body, then arms, then legs.

> To be able to start drawing a stick man, kids have to throw the toy or stone into a floor. Hit the lines of the skyscraper edges, or miss the skyscraper completely, and they don't get to draw.

> When each player manages to land the toy or stone into a floor of the skyscraper, they must start with the stick man's head, and write their initials in that head. (If you have different coloured chalks for each player writing initials is not necessary, but kids love doing this anyway.)

> Keep taking it in turns to throw and try to build your office workers.

> If you throw and the toy or stone lands on the roof in LONDON, then this is

like a Joker card. You can add a body part to any of your office workers!

> It may happen that players keep landing in different floors and end up building seven stick men at the same time. But encourage them to try to land where they have already drawn a head – and have a head start!

> Happy body-building everyone!

(In the traditional version of this game, you can only draw one arm or leg at a time. I allow my players to draw two arms at a time, and then two legs at a time, to avoid a prolonged game and keep it exciting. Also in the traditional version, the winner needs three stick men on the same floor. Forget that, it takes FOREVER. Three finished office workers anywhere in the building is enough for a victory!)

Let's Run With It...

Number of children needed: Two–lots

Age group: 4–10 years old

Preparation and energy required from grown-up: None

Duration: 5 minutes

Equipment: A sheet of newspaper for each child.

> Each competitor has a double page of a newspaper – a broadsheet, of course. And they have to read it. No, just kidding. They need to hold it flat across their tummy.

> Get them in a line, and on your count off they go. When you shout 'Go!' they must run as fast as they can with no hands on the paper. The object of the game is to see how far they can run before the newspaper falls off.

(This game obviously doesn't work on a windy day. And if it does work on a windy day, you know there has been some glue involved.)

Sheet Football

Number of children needed: Ten–lots (ten can include adults) plus an adult referee

Age group: 4–10 years old

Preparation and energy required from grown-up: None

Duration: 20 minutes

Equipment: Double duvet cover or large blanket, a football (but of the light variety) and a whistle for the referee.

This is a great party game, as it really focuses everyone's attention at the same time. Plus, to be honest, you need as many people as you can get your hands on. It's even well worth gatecrashing the neighbour's barbecue for this one.

> It is also a lot of fun for the oldies and the little ones at the same time – the oldies might need not to have back problems though as they will have to hold the pitch and steer the ball at the same height as the small ones do... But hey, it's football with no noisy kicking! Bliss!

> So, split your group into two teams. Or choose two captains and let them pick teams if that won't end up in too many tears!

> Let each team argue about which famous football team they are…

> Make each team elect a goalkeeper.

> Nominate or find a volunteer referee, who should of course have a whistle if possible.

> Place the duvet cover 'pitch' or large blanket onto the ground (sorry, but a single sheet will be too flimsy unless you are playing with a small beach ball and there is no wind at all).

> Put one team around the southern end and another team around the northern end. Place the goalkeeper in the middle of the southern and northern bits of the pitch.

> On the ref's count of three, everyone must pick up their little bit of the pitch and hold it waist high.

> The goalkeepers don't need to hold the pitch – they need their hands and heads.

> The game begins when the ref throws the ball into the middle of the pitch. The teams roll the ball towards the opposing goals by pulling their section of the sheet up and down!

Silly Races And Relays

Number of children needed: Four–lots

Age group: 4–10 years old

Preparation and energy required from grown-up: None

Duration: 20 minutes

Equipment: Apples or oranges, ping-pong balls or tennis balls, balls of socks, shoes, ice cubes, newspaper.

When it comes to races, there are more creative, more amusing and more original things to do than the traditional egg and spoon, three-legged and wheelbarrow races, for which you and your children have all got the 'been there, done that' T-shirt.

> Relay races and silly races are particularly good for birthday parties when you have a lot more children around, but hopefully not too many more!

> So here are a few more unusual and silly ideas for kids that will impress the other parents when you add the photos to that WhatsApp group.

▪ With apples or oranges on their backs, on all fours. A penalty point for each player or team is noted down for each time it falls off a player. (Sending them back to the start line makes it all go on for too long.)

- With a shoe on their tummy, wriggling on their backs or doing the crab. Again, penalty point scoring.

- Waddling with a ping-pong ball or tennis ball, like a penguin carrying an egg. If playing this as a relay, the ball must be transferred to the next player just as mummy and daddy penguins do it – with no hands.

- Pushing rolled-up balls of socks with their noses. But there must be no contact other than with the nose.

- Carrying ice cubes down their socks.

- Sliding with a sheet of newspaper under each foot (with socks on), without losing the newspaper (smooth surface required).

It's A Knockout

Number of children needed: Four–lots

Age group: 4–10 years old

Preparation and energy required from grown-up: None

Duration: 30 minutes

Equipment: Garden furniture, cardboard boxes.

A childhood is not a happy childhood without wonderful memories of the whole family humiliating themselves during a home-made obstacle course. I think we only did it once, inspired by the *It's a Knockout* TV show. We played it with our cousins but with most of the adults joining in, much to our delight.

> Small minds can recce the garden and help think of hilarious and challenging obstacles for the circuit, but an adult with their health and safety hat on needs to have the final say.

> So, you could make tunnels to crawl through using cardboard boxes, position sun loungers to make hurdles if you put them on their side (or for younger ones to

crawl under) and the garden hose could be set up as a limbo obstacle.

> You could also set up ball throwing challenges on the course using some buckets as nets.

> My dad was a sports teacher so, of course, he incorporated sit ups and press ups at various parts of the obstacle course, which was amusing mainly because we were all dressed up in crowns, capes and long dresses in homage to *It's a Royal Knockout*, which was such excruciatingly brilliant car crash TV to watch it simply had to be copied, plummy voices and all.

> The relay race ideas given previously can also be incorporated, as can balloons which must stay with each player until the end.

> Use a timer to score each player and issue penalty points when things go wrong. The one with the fastest time with the least penalty points wins, and any players who draw must be challenged again.

French Cricket

Number of children needed: Three players minimum

Age group: 6–10 years old

Preparation and energy required from grown-up: Almost none

Duration: 15 minutes

Equipment: Cricket bat and ball. If no cricket bat is available, it could be something similar like a folded umbrella or a tennis racquet.

French cricket is when you catch each other out by throwing a ball below the knee.

> The one with the bat makes a nice little pose with the bat held in front of the legs. The one with the ball throws it towards the batsman's legs.

> If the batsman hits the ball, they are able to move to another position (further away from the ball), but must freeze and take up the batting stance when the ball is picked up.

> If the batsman misses the ball they are not allowed to move.

> Whoever catches the ball becomes the next bowler from the spot they were in when they caught the ball. The batsman is out when the ball hits their legs.

> The lucky guy or girl who whacks the batsman below the knees is the next batsman.

Scoop Duel

Number of children needed: Two–lots

Age group: 4–10 years old

Preparation and energy required from grown-up: Cutting milk containers

Duration: 10 minutes

Equipment: Two plastic milk containers per duo playing – the ones with the handles. One tennis ball per duo. Good scissors or a knife.

If the children are not familiar with the concept of a duel, you will need to start by explaining this slightly drastic method of solving arguments from days gone by.

> Each player has a 'scoop' to throw the ball from, and catch the ball in, which is fashioned by cutting just above the handle of a plastic milk container. Smooth any sharp edges with a nail file or sandpaper before handing it to children.

> The game is played in pairs – hence the name 'Scoop Duel'.

> Flip a coin to find out who starts first with the ball in their scoop.

> Now, armed with their scoops, the two players must stand back to back.

> Next, they must solemnly, counting together, take five steps away from each other.

> On the fifth step, they must spin around and the player with the ball must launch it at their opponent, as if drawing a pistol in a duel.

> The opponent must catch the ball in their scoop; if they don't, they have lost a life. If they catch it, that person keeps the ball.

> They then both return to the start position and this time solemnly count six paces away from each other.

> And so on.

> The first person to lose five lives is the loser, and their duellist victorious!

(Explain how lucky they are to live in an era where people now just argue by super-fast texting on WhatsApp instead of shooting each other!)

Hot Potato

Number of children needed: Four players minimum

Age group: 4–10 years old

Preparation and energy required from grown-up: Revving them up!

Duration: 20 minutes

Equipment: A potato, a tennis ball or a ball of socks.

A classic and delicious bit of silliness, which just requires a bit of party spirit and preparation from the grown-up.

> Sit everyone in a circle, around arm stretches away from each other.

> For the first round or three, you need to be standing just outside the circle directing! (In later rounds this will be the oldest child while you enjoy a nice cup of tea or are busy with real potatoes.)

> Explain that the potato (or ball, or socks, pretending to be a potato) is BOILING HOT and that the idea is to quickly get rid of it when you catch it. Woe betide them

if they are holding the potato when you randomly shout 'HOT POTATO!', as they will be out!

> You start with the potato and throw it at someone in the circle – now close your eyes. Encourage fast throwing between players by shouting 'HOT, HOT, HOT'. After 30 seconds or so, shout 'HOT POTATO!'. Anyone holding it at that point is out.

> The reason your eyes are closed is to avoid accusations of favouritism or unfairness – the same thing happens in pass the parcel. This can be hard to do while policing the game. If you can see the children with the potato they will think you are trying to get them out. Another way of doing it is by standing outside the circle and just turning your back to them now and then when you shout 'HOT POTATO!'.

(As an alternative to shouting 'HOT POTATO!' you can use music – as in musical statues or musical chairs.)

Get Dressed (With A Balloon Race)

Number of children needed: Four players minimum—two per team

Age group: 5–10 years old

Preparation and energy required from grown-up: None

Duration: 20 minutes

Equipment: Balloons and lots of grown-up clothes.

You will definitely need the video camera on for this one as it is extremely amusing and very much one to keep for posterity. (The footage may also be useful to blackmail them when they are sulky teenagers by threatening to put it on Facebook.)

> First gather a selection of adult clothes. Like Noah you will need two of each kind, as this is a game for two teams – so two scarves, two grown-up shirts or similar, two hats, two pairs of boxer shorts, two bras, two skirts, two pairs of big socks (only if playing bare feet), etc.

> Now make your course. Make two piles of clothes a couple of feet away from each other, obviously with one of each kind of garment in each pile.

> Now create a start line at the other end of the lawn. (Best played on grass this, as falling over is an occupational hazard with this game.)

> Now hand each team a balloon. They must choose who goes first as this is a relay race. (If you have large teams, number them yourself to save arguments and time.)

> Now it's ready, steady, go – and they are off! Each player must keep their balloon in the air while running towards the pile of clothes. Each time a player gets to the pile of clothes they must grab a garment and put it on, while keeping the balloon in the air.

> If the balloon hits the ground, you have two options of scoring. Sending the player back to the start line, or docking seconds off their time. The latter works better if you have the energy to keep score!

(Children under eight can't usually flick the balloon high enough in the air for it to stay up long enough for them to put on an item of clothing, so the referee should help them flick the balloon – just every other flick that they do. Or just don't score and simply have fun!)

500

Number of children needed: Two–lots

Age group: 8–10 years old

Preparation and energy required from grown-up: None

Duration: 10 minutes

Equipment: A ball.

500 is a classic American game that adults with some numerical skills will enjoy, while feeling a tad worthy as a temporary maths teacher!

> In this game, the person who is 'it' stands about six feet from the other players, throws a ball into the air and calls out a number between 50 and 450. The player who catches the ball earns the number of points that the 'it' person called. However, if a player attempts to catch the ball and drops it, they lose the number of points announced. The first person to accumulate 500 points wins.

> Good luck and happy adding up!

Tails

Number of children needed: Four–lots

Age group: 4–10 years old

Preparation and energy required from grown-up: None

Duration: 20 minutes

Equipment: Nothing! If not playing on grass, maybe some spare socks or tea towels.

This is a cheeky little game of tag – but with a purpose! Stealing socks (or tails).

> If playing on a soft dry area, like grass, everyone sits down and takes their socks and shoes off, and then hangs one sock from their back pocket or waistband. This is their 'tail'.

> If it is not a good idea to take socks and shoes off, then supply everyone with a tail in the form of a spare sock, flannel or tea towel.

> Now mark out a pitch. It shouldn't be too big – about five square metres. The children shouldn't be able to get away from each other too easily!

> When everyone has a nice dinky little tail, it's time for the very simple fun to start.

> On the count of three they must run around trying to grab each other's tails, while trying not to let anyone grab theirs!

> When a player loses a tail, they must sit down. But although they are sitting down they can still try to grab at other people's tails and get back in the game – re-tailed!

> The last little one standing is the winner.

(This is a very cute bum-wiggling game.)

Make A Sundial

Number of children needed: Four–lots

Age group: 4–10 years old

Preparation and energy required from grown-up: None

Duration: 20 minutes

Equipment: Old umbrella or a parasol base. Large piece of white fabric, such as a sheet. Pencil and black marker pen.

You can use either of the following objects to make a sundial: an old umbrella opened up and placed upside down, or a defunct parasol base with a pole in it.

> Cut out a big circle on a white piece of fabric, around two metres in diameter for a parasol base; for the umbrella it depends on its size. This fabric is your 'clock'.

> Make a hole in the middle of the fabric so you can put the pole through it. Make sure the fabric is placed tightly. Use stones with the parasol holder, or staple it to your old umbrella.

> Get kids to write with a pencil first the times of the clock (for sure there will be mistakes the first time) and then

get them to write over the numbers with a thick black marker.

> Now let the sun do its work and rotate around the pole. Remind the kids to go and check the sundial a couple of times a day. They will love the sundial even more if they can draw their favourite activity for that specific hour on it (four o'clock eat a biscuit!, six o'clock watch their favourite TV programme).

Hunt The Pirate Flag

Number of children needed: Two–lots (or one plus you as a pirate)

Age group: 7–12 years old

Preparation and energy required from grown-up: Sourcing materials and policing

Duration: 25 minutes

Equipment: Long sticks, piece of fabric (size 40 x 40 cm), scissors, sticky tape, sewing kit, staplers, piece of cardboard, A4 paper, paints if you can handle the mess or if not, felt-tips!

You need to make two teams, because pirates need other pirates to steal things from. But you can have two teams of only one pirate each. Oh yes, me hearty!

> The first job for each team is to make its own flag. You can make this each team's very own challenge. Give the team its stick, fabric, and access to scissors, sewing stuff, sticky tape and a stapler...

> Each pirate team needs its own symbol. They can't both have skull and crossbones, but possibly one team could have the skull and the other one the crossbones. Or

they could be a dolphin team or a mermaid team... or a dinosaur team!

> So now it's paints or felt-tips out to make the flags...

> When the flags are ready to use, one team stays sequestered in the house while the other team goes to hide its flag in the garden. Absolutely no peeping allowed. When the first team has finished, the next team goes. They will love this secret stuff, but the peeping will need to be policed.

> With the flags hidden, it's time to give each team a piece of cardboard and tape an A4 piece of paper to it.

> Now each team has to draw a map on the cardboard to explain how to find its flag – with no spying; each team in different parts of the room!

> Maps give a game an extra dimension and it becomes real and more exciting. I love to play this game as well, and if you only have one child then obviously you can be the other pirate team.

> After five minutes, it's 'time up' and the teams have to swap maps.

> Who will be the first team to find the flag? The smartest ones of course...

Apples On String

Number of children needed: Two–lots, but they need to be of very similar height

Age group: 4–10 years old

Preparation and energy required from grown-up: Ten minutes or so. You do need to thread string through apples! As many apples as there are kids.

Duration: 10 minutes

Equipment: One apple per child. Thick cord or rope, similar to a washing line. Thick thread or typical (not chunky) string. A very large and long sewing needle with an eye large enough for the thread or string to go through.

> First, using the cord or rope, make a 'washing line' that you will hang the apples from using the thinner string or thread. The 'washing line' needs to be suspended one head above the head of the tallest child.

> You can do this using two trees or fences, or using the supports of swings in your play area.

> If you have a sliding scale of heights among your children, attach one end of the rope higher than the other end.

> Next you need to sew a piece of string through each apple, through the core. Start at the bottom end of the apple and push through to the top, where the stalk is. Tie a big knot in the string or thread at the bottom of the apple, so the apple sits on it, leaving a good long piece of string coming out at the top end of the apple. Don't cut it yet...

> You need the apples to dangle in front of the faces (especially mouths) of the little apple munchers. To do this properly, put the kids in position before you tie off the thread or string on the 'washing line'.

> Tie all the apples at equal intervals, at the right height for each child.

> Now for the rules! Tantalising apples ahead!

  1. No hands are to be used in this game.

  2. On the word 'Go' each player must choose an apple to eat. Hands free!

  3. The winner is the first player to eat their apple down to the core. (Or give them a time limit of five minutes and see who has eaten the most.)

> For children of six years old upwards the challenge of trying to eat the apple with no hands is great fun. Children under six will get frustrated after a few minutes, as it is actually quite difficult. Let them try with no hands for a minute, and then tell them that they can use one hand to touch the string above and below the apple, but not the apple itself.

(Don't forget to take some photos of the 'apples of your eye'!)

GAMES FOR THE GREAT OUTDOORS

Treasure Hunt

Number of children needed: Four–lots

Age group: 4–10 years old (but if you have a broad age range make sure you mix the younger ones with the older ones in each team, so that the little ones get plenty of help)

Preparation and energy required from grown-up: A fair bit, probably a couple of hours to prepare – but lots of glory to bask in when it goes well

Duration: 30 minutes or more depending on difficulty and number of clues

Equipment: Treasure, obviously, i.e. chocolate coins and sweets in a wooden box, and props if you play Version 2.

There are two ways, to my mind, to organise a treasure hunt.

Version 1

> Write clues that relate to the geography of where you are playing, e.g. 'Find the tallest tree and see what lies at the root of it'. You can write clues that ask players to count paces to the next one, or even take coordinates and use a compass, etc.

Version 2

> Write clues that are riddles and relate to props, such as, 'What gets wetter the more it dries?' (which is a towel of course, and the next clue will be under it). Note this is a good option if you think there is a chance your outdoor treasure hunt might get rained off, as you can transfer this one inside.*

> If you have two or more teams, the secret of a good treasure hunt is to have all the kids back at base deciphering the last clue to where the treasure is, together. It's not a pretty sight if one team gets stuck and another races to the treasure and commences gorging on chocolate while the others are crying.

> To avoid this, make sure that the last clue is a communal effort and the teams need each other to decipher the final clue to the hiding place. One way of doing this is to arrange for each team to have its own set of clues, and on the back of each clue write a word that is part of the final 'communal' clue, which they must all keep hold of. All the words together make up the last clue, which the teams must work out together when they are all back at base camp.

> The penultimate clue for each team should also lead back to base camp.

> Start both teams off at this base camp and explain the rules properly to them.

(And yes, you do deserve some of that chocolate. The most work of all the games in this book. Well done.)

* There are more riddles in the 'Games For On the Move' section at the end of this book.

Spider Web

Number of children needed: Four–lots

Age group: 4–10 years old

Preparation and energy required from grown-up: Quite a bit! But worth it.

Duration: 20 minutes

Equipment: Balls of wool in as many different colours as there are kids.

Often played indoors at the cost of smashed vases and collapsing furniture, this well-known American game is much better played in the park or the woods than inside. Saves your Ming vases (or, OK, IKEA ones).

> You need to find a cluster of trees that are close to each other and that don't have too many low-lying branches at the kids' eye level, so they are safe. You can also use other things that are around like a gate, fencing or picnic tables. Just be aware of other park users so that you don't annoy anybody...

> Now you need to start spinning a giant spider web with the different balls of wool. Use one colour at a time so

they go in different directions, but you do want them overlapping each other as much as possible, so that it looks more like an actual spider's web and will be more challenging to unravel.

> You need to choose the same place to end each ball of wool, after you have wound it around trunks and branches (that aren't too high for the kids to reach) along with any other objects. This is where your little spiders (or is it the revenge of the flies?) will start their de-webbing.

> So now it is time for the game to commence. Give each spider (or fly) a colour (don't let them choose a colour or they will still be arguing until sunset – you know what kids are like about colours...) and on the count of three off they go, each racing to be the first to unravel their bit of the giant web.

> The first player to untangle their ball of wool is the winner.

(Don't forget to video this as they will love to watch it back.)

What's The Time, Mr Wolf?

Number of children needed: Four–lots

Age group: 4–10 years old

Preparation and energy required from grown-up: None

Duration: 10 minutes

Equipment: None

So first of all, tell the little ones that you are a wolf and they are chickens. Make sure they know you are a very hungry wolf (you haven't had any dinner for days) and they are going to need to be very fast-moving chickens when you decide that it is 'DINNER TIME!'.

> Choose a den for each game – it could be behind a fallen log or behind a tree. This is the safe area that the chickens can run to before the wolf can catch them.

> Now they need to follow you from a short distance while asking the question, 'What's the time, Mr Wolf?'. You reply with random times like 'one o'clock', 'two o'clock', 'midnight', 'half past five', etc. – keep the suspense going for about six replies, until you shout 'DINNER TIME!' at

which point they must run like the wind as you try to catch them.

> The first chicken you catch becomes the wolf. Be strict about this, because they usually all want to be the wolf and you don't want a fight on your hands. If, like me, you can't often catch one (children are surprisingly fast when they are pretending to be in fear of being eaten by a wolf while giggling their heads off), then have a rule to decide who will be the wolf next, e.g. oldest first.

Manhunt

Number of children needed: Four–lots

Age group: 7–10 years old

Preparation and energy required from grown-up: Sourcing equipment and explaining the rules

Duration: 20 minutes

Equipment: Camouflage-coloured clothing, a blindfold or scarf, face paints.

This is basically Cops and Robbers – or in this version because you are in the great outdoors, Cops and Fugitives.

> In preparation at home, the players need to camouflage themselves by wearing dark green, brown and black. If available, get the face paints out and get them to use the same colours on their faces and hands.

> Time to head to a nice wooded park where there are lots of trees – and ideally no other families relaxing that you might annoy.

> On arrival you need to choose two spots opposite each other, separated by about ten metres. One should be christened 'Base Camp' and the other 'Jail'.

> Now, use the argument-avoiding-method of a counting out chant, 'ip dip...' and the last player to be 'let go' is pronounced the Cop for the first game.

> The others are Fugitives and now have a good five minutes to hide themselves. The Cop should not be allowed to watch where they go, so will need blindfolding.

> Before they go off into hiding, you will need to explain the rules of the game, as they are not that simple!

> Once the Fugitives are in their excellent hiding places (up trees, behind fallen logs, covered head to foot in leaves, etc.) then it is time to unleash the Cop.

> So, the objectives are as follows...

  1. Cop must now find and tag the Fugitives and get them into Jail.

  2. The Fugitives must try to get to Base Camp without being tagged.

> To arrest a Fugitive the Cop has to lift a Fugitive off the ground, by putting their arms around the Fugitive's waist and announcing 'You're under arrest'.

> Now the arrested Fugitive, tail between their legs, has to RUN to the Jail.

> The reason I say they have to RUN is that the Fugitives, if they tag anyone else who has been arrested, can free them by tagging them.

> Same system – the tagged Fugitive has to be held aloft and the tagging Fugitive must utter the words 'You are free to go'. Then of course the arrested Fugitive simply becomes a Fugitive again.

> So, how to score or adjudicate.

1. If all the Fugitives get to Base Camp they win the round. The last person back is the next Cop.

2. However, if there are four Fugitives at Base Camp and one in Jail, the team will decide if they want to end the round or try to tag the other Fugitive out of Jail but, in doing so, risk getting out too.

(If they decide that they want to end the round there, it's a fair cop!)

Pooh Sticks

Number of children needed: One–lots

Age group: 4–10 years old

Preparation and energy required from grown-up: None

Duration: 10 minutes

Equipment: A river, stream or brook with a bridge – and sticks!

I don't know how many hours of my life as a child in Devon I spent playing this with my brothers and sisters. Finding a new bridge on an outing was like having a surprise bonus birthday.

> The idea is that each player must find a stick and throw it simultaneously with the other players' off the bridge, from the upstream side. Then each player quickly crosses the bridge to track their stick's progress and see whose stick has won the race.

> We used to customise our sticks by shredding any twigs and making them streamlined.

> And repeat, and repeat, and repeat!

> Nothing more therapeutic than gazing into babbling brooks. Well, apart from Netflix. Or reading *Winnie The Pooh*.

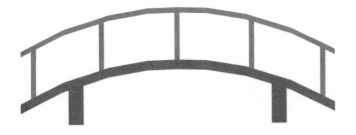

Leaf Catcher

Number of children needed: One–lots

Age group: 4–10 years old

Preparation and energy required from grown-up: None

Duration: 20 minutes

Equipment: A basket, bucket or bag for each player to catch leaves in and a stopwatch. This game needs to be played in woodland.

Autumn is best for this woodland game of course, in which within a five-minute timeframe each leaf catcher must collect the most leaves.

> Each player must first scour the landscape for windfall (leaves).

> Each player can BAGSIE three areas that they think they can find the most booty in – so they say from 'THAT TREE to THAT TREE' and pace it out. Each player, duo or team commandeers their patch.

> Press the stopwatch and let them find their booty!

› Grown-up: count leaves and award a trophy!

(While you have their attention, it's a good time to teach them the names of those trees. There must be an app for that...)

Making Fairy Homes

Number of children needed: One–lots

Age group: 4–7 years old – or older if they still believe in fairies

Preparation and energy required from grown-up: None

Duration: 30 minutes

Equipment: Garden twine.

This is one for your little aspiring builders or architects.

> Gather the troops and explain that you have heard on the grapevine (yes, Mummy may have had some wine with her friends last night) that you have heard there is a shocking housing shortage among the fairy population and that help is needed to construct some tiny little fairy homes. Or, if you really want to get authentic, fake a message in a bottle from the fairies and plant it in the garden for the children to find themselves.

> Once the message has been received, get the children to find their smallest dolls or figurines (legs-up-to-armpits-Barbie is way too supermodel-esque for this game) and explain that they should take these little guys along to test out the new houses.

> Get them to do a head count and also explain that the dollies will all need to come home, as nobody leaves plastic in the woods.

> When you arrive at your destination – a lovely park or woodland – get the children to help you identify some plots for building teeny tiny houses, such as nice trees with roots.

> Once the location has been sourced, despatch them to collect building materials, within your sight. Tell them that leaves might make nice front doors, moss might become nice thatched-style roofs, twigs can be garden gates, bright green grass might make nice carpets, acorns might be cool vase decorations or even washing machines for little fairy clothes. Stones can be ovens for baking bread and cakes. You get the drift.

> Stand by to help twine together tiny twigs to make little garden gates and fences.

> When the houses are looking good you can pretend to be an estate agent and value them.

> Now sit back on a nice rug and relax while they play in the tiny homes with their dollies.

> When you want to go home, pretend you just got an email from the fairies who have just

told you that they need to move in straight away! But, of course, they need to do it secretly.

> If any of the kids don't want to budge, remind them that fairies don't like to be seen. And down payment on their new houses can only be made in little tiny magical tears of relief. No fairy wants anyone to see that.

(Plus if they are seen, they can't do their very important work with small teeth...)

You Animals!

Number of children needed: One–lots

Age group: 6–10 years old

Preparation and energy required from grown-up: A 20-minute rehearsal, but this is part of the game

Duration: 60 minutes

Equipment: None

The preparation for this game might require some online research, unless Grandad happens to be David Attenborough.

> Can your little ones imitate an elephant accurately, or make a sound like a vulture? Or a meerkat? Or a lion roaring? Can they howl like a wolf or growl like a bear? Or sing like a penguin, chatter like a dolphin or crow like a cockerel?

> The research part of this game is all part of the fun. Each player needs to look on the internet for examples of some more unusual animal sounds and practise imitating them. This is a giggle to do and great to 'up the ante' for the game, rather than just all sounding like cats and dogs!

> Animal sounds learned and shared, it is time to head to the woods.

> Essentially this is a woodland version of Marco Polo, also known as Animal Echo.

> Draw straws or use your preferred method of deciding who gets to be the Animal Caller first.

> The other players must then all hide in different places in the woods. Not spread too far apart though, as everyone must be within earshot of each other.

> Now the Animal Caller must choose one of their newly-learned animal sounds.

> The other players must echo the sound and recreate it. The Animal Caller uses the sounds to locate players and chase them through the woods.

> The first person tagged becomes the next Animal Caller.

> T'wit t'woooo! (Yep, nothing like a real owl!)

Frisbee™ Golf

Number of children needed: Two–lots

Age group: 7–10 years old

Preparation and energy required from grown-up: Design of a golf course

Duration: 10 minutes

Equipment: Frisbee, pen and paper to keep score.

This is pretty much as it sounds in the title, but with a Frisbee as opposed to golf balls and clubs.

> First you will need to design your very own 'golf course' for Frisbee playing. And then play an extended and purposeful Frisbee session, scoring yourselves as you would when playing golf or mini golf.

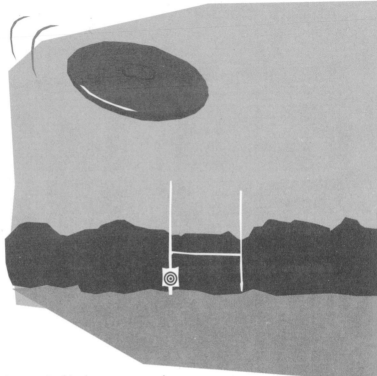

> Instead of holes, you need to create targets. These can be simply jumpers or coats, or paper signs, or towels, spread out to their full extent. To end each 'hole' in golf lingo, the Frisbee must land on the target.

> Frisbee Golf works best in wide open spaces. It must be a space that doesn't see many people, and there should always be a spotter to stop the game if members of the public appear on the horizon.

> It is also great if there are some hazards in the way, e.g. small bushes, the odd tree, bunkers.

> To spice things up you can also spin players around five times before they take their first throw, so that they are dizzy.

> But the real point of the game is to see which person in the team can hit the targets with the least amount of throws. And if anyone can get a 'jumper in one'!

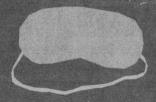

GAMES FOR THE POOL

Most of these games would not be allowed in public pools in the UK but if you are lucky enough to have access to a private pool, or go abroad and have a holiday where you get to use a pool, then these games are for you... AN ADULT MUST BE PRESENT AT ALL TIMES! And sorry, but all of these games are only suitable for confident swimmers who can swim without armbands.

Shark Tails

Number of children needed: Two–lots

Age group: Confident swimmers

Preparation and energy required from grown-up: None

Duration: 10 minutes

Equipment: Just the pool.

I made this game up for my daughter immediately after we had watched the brilliant film *Shark Tale*. As the credits rolled, we rolled out of our cinema-bed and relocated to our communal pool, where we pretended to be sharks. After a few minutes, our favourite game in this book was born.

> Each player is a shark. Each player has a turn to announce three (human) parts of the body – e.g. elbow, nose, tummy, knee, shoulder, chin, head, foot – or bum (known as the shark's tail). On the count of three, each player must try to touch each of these parts of the other players – in no particular order. The first player to manage to touch or gently tap the three different parts of the same player, usually underwater of course, wins a point.

> The reason why it's so much fun is you can try to sabotage the other player or players by wriggling the part they need to win away from them. There is something very entertaining about the speechlessness of the game when underwater.

> This game doesn't get rough as it is all about grappling underwater but it is a good idea to make sure nobody needs their nails cut and nobody is wearing chunky jewellery.

> Don't forget to keep score and win an ice cream or a night off from the washing-up.

Sharks And Minnows

Number of children needed: Two–lots

Age group: Confident swimmers

Preparation and energy required from grown-up: None

Duration: 10 minutes

Equipment: Just the pool.

A famous classic, but here it is in case you have forgotten the rules.

> Choose the deep end of a large pool.

> The game starts with one person selected as the shark and the rest as the minnows.

> Again, if you don't want World War Three on your holiday, use bits of paper in the sun hat, with as many bits of paper as players, and with only one having a scary pair of teeth on it representing the shark.

> The shark starts in the water on one side of the pool (of course, they are the boss) and the minnows usually start on the deck of the other side.

> The game starts by the shark calling out 'Sharks and minnows, one two three, fishies, fishies swim to me!' from one end of the pool, at which point the minnows start from the other end of the pool, shake a leg and dive in to swim to the opposite end of the pool.

> If the shark manages to tag a minnow before said minnow touches the wall, then that minnow becomes a shark in the next round.

> After all the minnows have either reached the wall or been tagged, the shark(s) swim to the other wall and the cycle starts all over again.

> If some of the minnows refuse to enter the pool, the shark may swim to the other wall and tag it – whoever was still out of the pool when the shark tags the wall becomes a shark.

> The game is played until all of the minnows have been tagged. Naturally.

(IMPORTANT RULE for avoiding arguments... it is the first person who was tagged that becomes the shark in the next game.)

Marco Polo

Number of children needed: Two–lots

Age group: Confident swimmers

Preparation and energy required from grown-up: None

Duration: 10 minutes

Equipment: A blindfold that works when wet.

This is a hugely popular game that really needs to be kept alive through the generations – and this certainly wouldn't be a good section on pool games without this classic.

> One player is blindfolded and is Polo. The others must swim around Polo and when Polo shouts 'Marco!', the other players are supposed to shout 'Polo!', so Polo can swim towards them and tag them.

> It can be tricky to organise the blindfold but little pieces of an old towel stuffed into goggles works well. And you do need to police the game as the ones closest to Polo tend to go quiet, other than the odd giggle…

> When all players are tagged, the first player to have been tagged becomes Marco Polo.

> Alternatively, you can set a time limit so that nobody gets bored and just take turns.

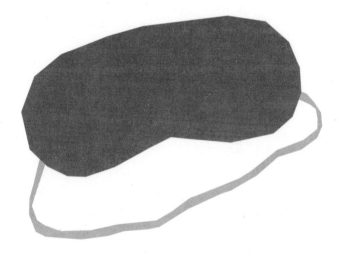

Dive For It

Number of children needed: Two–lots

Age group: Confident swimmers

Preparation and energy required from grown-up: None

Duration: 10 minutes

Equipment: Coins (lots of them) and other objects to hand that sink. Two 1.5-litre plastic bottles with lids.

> First fill up the water bottles with water and put the lids on, then make your little fishes turn away so they can't see you throw the water bottles into the water. Then they look, they squint, they try to find the glistening bottles blending in with the bottom of the pool… They dive, they retrieve – first one back up is victorious.

> Do the same with coins. Turn the kids away before you fling your last coins into the pool and then watch for the treasure to be found. May the best pirate win!

> If you have lots of swimmers, put them into two teams and throw in (while they look away) sets of identical things that sink, such as coins and seashells. Each team starts at opposite sides and it's the team that gets one of each thing out first that wins.

Ping-Pong Madness

Number of children needed: Two–lots

Age group: Confident swimmers

Preparation and energy required from grown-up: None

Duration: 10 minutes

Equipment: Lots of ping-pong balls and an indelible pen.

Grasping ping-pong balls bobbing about while racing another player is about as good as it gets. And a good fun fitness class for grown-ups.

> Write in permanent markers the name of each player on a split proportion of the ping-pong balls you have. So, if you have 20 balls and five players, write each name on four balls.

> Then throw the ping-pong balls into the water and let the slippery-grippery madness begin! They need to find all the ones with their names on.

> They also need to get their ping-pong balls out of the pool, too, as it's not easy swimming with ping-pong balls stashed about your person... and so we elaborate on

this game by having each player throw their ping-pong balls from the water into their own bucket or bowl, or towels suspended between sun loungers to make nets.

The Crazy Melon Game

Number of children needed: Two–lots

Age group: Confident swimmers

Preparation and energy required from grown-up: None

Duration: 30 minutes

Equipment: A small honeydew melon and lots of petroleum jelly.

> Grease up a small melon with the petroleum jelly. Have each player at a corner of the pool.

> A grown-up will now need to throw the slippery melon into the centre of the pool.

> The objective of the game is for the players to get to it first (or steal it from whoever does) and swim back to their home corner pushing the tricky melon, then get the thing out of the pool.

> Half an hour killed, with a lot of giggles.

> Be careful. Although this game is hysterical, a melon is not a beach ball. DON'T throw it at each other's heads! And make sure one adult is being lifeguard in case that happens.

(Mums, best not mention this game to the pool guy, no matter how good looking and friendly he is... he won't like grease in the pool. Plus, the melon might split and you don't want to be held responsible. It's a 'just once this holiday' kind of game!)

Shoulder Fights With Mites

Number of children needed: Four, or two kids plus two adults. Or the more the merrier – but no odd numbers.

Age group: Confident swimmers

Preparation and energy required from grown-up: None

Duration: 10 minutes

Equipment: Just the pool.

You probably all know this one. Each adult (or older child) has a child (or smaller child) on their shoulders and it becomes a fight to the death... well OK, not death, but toppling over.

> Each player on top pushes, pulls and shoves to 'destabilise' the opposition. And this is how you will win the game.

> One point is earned for each pair that topples the opposition.

> Mum should be refereeing from a lounger and taking photos. Kids never look as cute as they do when they

are all wet and shiny, or are as lovely and quiet as they are when they are busy swimming underwater having the time of their lives.

(IMPORTANT TIP – Be firmly in charge of deciding which peeps should be on top to avoid inappropriate weight or heights that could cause injury.)

Water Rounders

Number of children needed: Ideally two teams of five, which can be a combination of kids and adults, but there are ways of making this work with fewer people and a smaller circuit

Age group: Confident swimmers

Preparation and energy required from grown-up: Finding, buying or borrowing a beach ball

Duration: 10 minutes

Equipment: Beach ball.

Assign two teams among your water babies and grown-ups.

> This game works well in a pool that's not too big, so let's hope your villa isn't too fancy. Otherwise block off half the pool as best you can… maybe some butlers can help you!

> Create a 'home base' in the middle of the wall in the shallow end. Mark it with a T-shirt or a towel, then make four further bases: two on the corners on the left and right of the shallow end, and two more on the remaining corners – so you make a square circuit.

> As in rounders, one team has to bat and the other team has to field.

> The batting team puts its first player in the pool at the 'home base' and the rest of the players line up out of the pool behind them.

> The fielding team spreads out around the pool. Each individual 'fielder' must catch the ball whenever it is flung nearest to them and then swim in a big hurry towards the base that the 'batter' is nearest to, to try to get them out – so ideally, each team has a fielder treading water or hanging onto the side of the pool close to each of the four corner bases. Toss a coin to decide which team bats first.

> It's important to use a beach ball as it should not fly too far, essentially, or be hit outside the pool, because then you are into problems with 'slippy slidy' feet.

> To eliminate the batter, the fielding team must either catch the ball and try to hit the batter while they swim between bases, or throw the ball to hit the actual base that the batter is en route to.

> Points are awarded for each full circuit of the pool completed – when a batter makes it all the way back to the home base without being hit by the beach ball, or having the base they were approaching hit. They can pause at any base while the next batting player takes their turn.

> The person throwing the beach ball to the batter must stand in the shallow end fairly close to the batter – beach balls don't travel as well as other balls!

> The 'bat' used is one or both hands, as in volleyball.

GAMES FOR
THE BEACH

Panuelo
(Or The Hanky Game)

Number of children needed: You need at least four on each side, so eight in total. Can be a mix of children and adults, plus an adult in charge of the hanky… so this is a game for when you are on holiday with another family or have made some very good friends

Age group: 5–10 years old and adults

Preparation and energy required from grown-up: No prep, just finding a hanky, a T-shirt or borrowing a tea towel from the hotel, villa or bar

Duration: 15 minutes

Equipment: Hanky, T-shirt or tea towel.

This is a donkeys-old mucho, mucho fun Spanish game.

> The grown-up in charge needs a hanky, T-shirt or tea towel (a beach towel or sarong is too big) and also a loud voice and steady feet as they will be flung upon from two directions. So maybe not Gran – even if she has been annoying this holiday…

> So the Hanky Adult puts two teams opposite each other, standing in a line facing each other (a horizontal line, not behind each other) about four metres apart.

> The Hanky Adult now gives each team member a number, with both teams getting the same numbers, e.g. each team has a number one, a number two, a number three, etc. Up to the number of players in each team.

> It doesn't matter whether the number ones, etc. are facing each other, you can mix it up – so number two isn't necessarily standing between number one and number three. What is important is that each person learns their number. Trust me, it will probably be the grown-ups that forget.

> Now Hanky Adult stands halfway between the two teams – but not in the middle, at the side.

> Now they shout a number – say 'THREE'.

> Both the number threes from each team must race to grab the hanky from the adult, who stays still throughout the game. The first to grab it must run back to their team with it to get a point.

> HOWEVER… until the number three with the hanky gets back to their cheering team, they are still fair game to the other number three, who can rugby tackle them for that hanky, or tickle them so they drop it, or just rip it out of their hands and get that hanky back to their own home team. Yes, brutal but fun.

> Hanky Adult keeps score of the number of times each team secures the hanky.

(They will need a beer or glass of wine after this game.)

Variations for Hanky Adult To shout

> HA can shout two numbers at the same time, who must hold hands on their way to the hanky. So 2 and 4 must find each other as they leave the line and approach the hanky holding hands.

> HA can shout two numbers at the same time, who must piggy back their way to the hanky. (Good idea for the smallest one to be on top.)

> HA can shout 'HOP!' and two numbers, so hopping is required.

> HA can shout 'BACKWARDS!', so a backwards approach is required. (Definitely have the camera ready for this one.)

> 'ON ALL FOURS!', 'ON YOUR TUMMY!', 'ON YOUR BEHIND!' are all good ones to have the beach chuckling at the mad Brits, too. Unless you are in Spain, where they will have seen it all before…

Shark And Fish

Number of children needed: About eight children really, but adults can play too

Age group: 5–10 years old

Preparation and energy required from grown-up: None

Duration: 15 minutes

Equipment: None

This is a traditional Chinese game called Cat and Mouse, but that's too tame... this is the bolder beach version.

> One player is chosen to be a shark (the chaser, humming the *Jaws* tune) and another one gets to mouth bubbles a lot, and be a little fish.

> If you want to avoid arguments, especially on a beach with more well-behaved families watching, then use bits of paper chucked in a sun hat where you have written 'Shark' and 'Fish' on just two of them for players to pull out of the hat.

> The rest of the team forms a circle holding hands, with the fish INSIDE the circle, and the shark outside.

> Now the gang in the circle moves around while calling out the following rhyme:

  - 'What time is it?'

  - 'Just struck nine.'

  - 'Is the shark around?'

  - 'He's about to dine.'

> When the charming little ditty ends, the circle freezes, legs wide apart, and the shark starts to chase the fish, weaving in and out of the sandy legs to do so – if adults are in the circle, they might need to be on their knees.

> CRUCIAL RULE… the shark MUST follow the fish's path. Precisely!

> When they catch the fish they can enjoy pretending to 'eat' them, and then it's time for another round.

(Of the game, I said… not the Sangria…)

Buckets, Balls And Good Throwers!

Number of children needed: One–lots

Age group: 3–8 years old

Preparation and energy required from grown-up: 6 minutes

Duration: 20–25 minutes

Equipment: Three empty buckets of different sizes and anything that is big and easy to throw (stones, beach balls, coins, sun cream tubes, toys), plus objects that are small and very difficult to throw (straws, feathers or leaves).

Let kids get a collection of buckets, ideally from their own stock and some boxes blagged from the local beach restaurant. Different sizes are what you are after. And then ask them to find the things that they will need to throw (as mentioned above).

> Put the buckets or boxes in a horizontal line. The first box is the biggest and gives the players only ten points. The next one is bit smaller and gives them 20 points, and as you can guess... the last one is much smaller and gives the players 30 points.

> Now everybody takes turns to throw the 'balls' one at a time into the buckets/boxes.

(It's interesting, psychologically, to observe your little ones when they play this game. Some will play very safe and go for the easy scores, and some will live dangerously, playing high risk for maximum points. Their futures unfold a little in front of you...)

Towel Ball

Number of children needed: Four per game

Age group: 4–10 years old

Preparation and energy required from grown-up: None

Duration: 10 minutes

Equipment: Beach ball and large towels.

Towel Ball is similar to volleyball but without the need for a net. And it's lots of fun as there is always lots of falling over.

> Draw a nice square pitch in the sand, about half the size of a shrunken volleyball court, with a line down the middle in place of a net. Roughly four square metres in total.

> Each pair of players hold each short end of a beach towel, creating a kind of cradle between them. Obviously, put the pairs together based on similar heights if possible.

> The idea is to throw the ball pair to pair, from towel to towel.

> It takes a bit of practice!

> Score very simply. If a team doesn't manage to scoop up the ball in its towel when thrown, and it drops onto the sand, then that team is given a 'negative' point. The first team to gain ten 'negative' points loses the match.

(Be aware that you will be having so much fun that other random sunbathers will be putting down their books and wanting a tournament before the day is out.)

What Good Drivers!

Number of children needed: Two–lots

Age group: 4–8 years old

Preparation and energy required from grown-up: A fair bit, but the children definitely do the running around for once

Duration: 15 minutes

Equipment: None

Find a decent space on the beach where you won't annoy anyone!

> Then ask your children if they know how to drive a car. They will of course say yes.

> Tell them that you are about to turn into a very strict policeman.

> Next you need to teach them the instructions and the actions that follow them:

1. Green – Go! They must drive – i.e. run around and make revving sounds like a car.

2. Yellow – wait for the lights to change. Demonstrate by pacing on the spot, rolling your eyes and looking at your watch.

3. Red – Stop! They must freeze. Last one to freeze is eliminated by you.

4. Reverse. They must drive backwards. Anyone who crashes into someone else is eliminated.

5. Roundabout. They must drive in tight circles. Always amusing re dizzy factor.

6. Park. They must sit down in a line in front of you. Last one to sit down is eliminated by you.

7. Broken down. They must sit down and lie back and kick their legs (wheels) in the air. Nice on the sand.

8. Crash. They have to bump into each other, tummy to tummy while saying 'CRASH!'

> If they are old enough to understand left and right, or need to practise it, then you can add 'turn right' and 'turn left' instructions.

> Now start the game. Change the instructions every 10 – 30 seconds and eliminate the last player to follow the instruction or those who get it wrong.

> Initially you will need to demonstrate this game with a bit of gusto, then when the game starts you can have a

little sit down on your towel and just bark the orders or promote a child to be the traffic light.

> The more kids with this one the more fun, as you can go to town more with eliminating.

(TIP – Don't worry about potential tantrums for getting eliminated. Most kids actually love to be 'caught'. A reassuring affirmation of the innate naughtiness of the human race.)

On The Ball, On The Beach

Number of children needed: About eight children, but adults can play too

Age group: 4–10 years old

Preparation and energy required from grown-up: None

Duration: 15 minutes

Equipment: A beach ball, volleyball, basketball or football.

Everyone literally needs to be on the ball for this one, so maybe not to be played after a long lunch...

> Stand the team in a circle with a ball.

> The ball is thrown quickly around and across the circle. Each time the ball is skilfully caught, the peeps on either side of the catcher must put one arm up in air – the arm nearest the person with the ball – and hold that arm in the air until the ball is thrown again.

> Obviously if any one drops the ball or doesn't put the correct arm up, they are DISQUALIFIED...

> Play until there is only one left standing... the ice cream winner.

> If this game is played fast it is great fun, as confusion reigns. But maybe start slow so they don't lose interest and complain.

Hop Sticks

Number of children needed: Two–lots

Age group: 5–10 years old and adults too

Preparation and energy required from grown-up:
Collecting lovely driftwood sticks, around 12 inches long, so you need a beach that has that… unless you have prepared back at the ranch

Duration: 15 minutes

Equipment: None

This game is Hopscotch without the stress of the numbers.

> Time for a lovely long walk to scour the beach and any dunes for lovely driftwood sticks (that they can turn into a cool photo frame for you one day with a bit of wood glue…).

> If you have two players, they need ten sticks each. Or if you have many mites, or the adults are joining in, you need ten sticks per team.

> Now each player or team needs to make a ladder on the sand with the sticks, each rung about one adult footstep apart.

> One player from each team starts, hopping over the sticks without touching any of them. If a stick is stepped on the player is disqualified.

> When the player has hopped over all the sticks, they stop, still on one foot, and bend down to pick up the last stick – Hopscotch style. They then hop back to base over the remaining sticks.

> Reaching the beginning again, they drop the stick and set off again to hop over the nine remaining sticks, pick up the last one, and back to base.

> Keep them at it until all of the sticks have been picked up.

> A player is also disqualified if they put both feet on the sand at the same time.

> With just two playing, the winner is the player who finishes with the least mistakes.

> With two teams playing, the winner is the team which has got the furthest along when all players are disqualified. If both teams finish, the winning team is the one which finishes with the most players left.

Variations

Play as a relay. The first player hops over ten sticks, returning with the tenth. The second player hops over nine, the third hops over eight, etc. This works very well with mixed age groups, where the younger children play towards the end of the team's go.

Beach Minigolf

Number of children needed: Two–lots

Age group: 5–10 years old

Preparation and energy required from grown-up: Very little

Duration: 15 minutes

Equipment: A golf club which can be an upside-down umbrella and a ball of some sort.

Self-explanatory really for anyone who has ever played minigolf and fun for those of you who are creative.

> Challenge the young Colin Montgomery(s) to make a five-hole minigolf course that is as elaborate as possible and remind them that they might make some friends on the beach when the super cool golf course is finished.

> This is so much better than just letting them bury you, because they will be busy for ages, you get to sunbathe without sand all over you and later you get to have a round (of golf!).

> The kids will need fairly wet sand to make nice little courses so if the sand is dry you will need to make it wet

but that shouldn't be too hard if you have a container for transporting sea water.

> Suggest they build bridges and short tunnels – maybe one shaped like an octopus and one that ends in a shark's mouth. Perhaps a mini helter-skelter formed from a little hill with grooves running down it.

> They might need to hunt down some sticks and shells for engineering and decoration, and they can use any props they can find. Straws and cocktail umbrellas make great flags for the holes.

> Bliss for you while the work is in progress as long as you look up from your e-book and say 'Wow!' now and then or chip in with the odd idea.

The Gymnastics Tournament

Number of children needed: One–lots

Age group: 6–10 years old

Preparation and energy required from grown-up: None

Duration: 15 minutes

Equipment: None

Gymnastics used to be a girly thing when I was young, but more and more boys are loving it these days. Maybe they are realising what chick magnets they will turn out to be.

> Give each of your springy offspring a beach towel and tell them to make the most of the lovely soft sand to practise their best yet gymnastics 'on the floor (beach)' routine. Tell them you want to see lots of perfect roly-polies, handstands, flips and graceful landings and dancing.

> When they are ready to reveal their hard work, make sure you give them a 10. They are on holiday, after all.

GAMES FOR
ON THE MOVE
IN CARS, PLANES
AND TRAINS

True Or False?

> **Number of children needed:** One–lots
>
> **Age group:** 6–12 years old
>
> **Preparation and energy required from grown-up:** None
>
> **Duration:** Depends but at least 20 minutes
>
> **Equipment:** None

If you like the brilliant comedy TV programme *Would I Lie to You?* and have learned a little bit from the masters about pretending that a lie is a truth and vice versa, then you can have a lot of fun with this.

> You can either do this by telling remarkable real-life or made-up stories from your past, or (if your life has been quite dull or you just can't remember any of the mad things that happened to you before you became a parent) then you can just use the list of myths and facts below.

> For the former version, the grown-up either has to tell a slightly unbelievable true story and make it sound even more unbelievable when they tell it, or make up an unrealistic story and make it sound quite realistic. Next, the rest of the passengers ask questions to try to figure

out if it is true or false. After three questions – one from each member of the guessing team – it's time to declare whether the story really happened or is a bluff.

For the version with myths and facts, here are some good ones. (Don't let the people you are playing with see this page if they can read or know that T stands for True and F stands for Big Fat Porky-Pie!)

A giraffe can clean its ears with its tongue. (T) A giraffe's tongue is 21 inches long.

Lightning never strikes the same place twice. (F) The Empire State Building gets hit about a hundred times a year.

If you get stung by a jellyfish, it helps if you wee on it. (F) It actually releases more venom!

Dolphins sleep with one eye open. (T)

All penguins mate for life. (F)

Fresh vegetables are healthier than frozen ones (F) Often there are more nutrients in frozen vegetables if they are frozen quickly after picking.

More people are killed by bees than snakes. (T)

If you swallow chewing gum, it takes seven years to digest it! (F) It will be digested normally, like other food.

Elephants know when they are close to death, and make their way to a place known as the elephants' graveyard. (F)

An ostrich's eye is bigger than its brain. (T)

Slugs have four noses. (T)

Goldfish only have a three-second memory. (F)

Bulls get angry when they see red. (F) They are actually colour-blind. It's the cape waving they hate!

It's dangerous to wake sleepwalkers up. (F)

It is impossible to sneeze with your eyes open. (T)

If You're Happy And You Know It...

Number of children needed: One–lots

Age group: 4–8 years old

Preparation and energy required from grown-up: None

Duration: 10 minutes

Equipment: None

This song is a good one to customise on long journeys with one child, or lots, aged between four and eight. Have them make up their own alternatives to the boring old 'clap your hands' or 'stamp your feet' and invent silly mimes with sound effects for each lyric.

> These are our favourites…

> Do a dance, sing a song, pick your nose, scratch your bum, have a cuddle, walk the dog, have a swim, ride your bike, eat an ice cream, tell a joke, kiss your mum.

Little Boxes

Number of children needed: One–lots

Age group: 5–12 years old

Preparation and energy required from grown-up: Making sure you have paper, pens and something to lean the paper on

Duration: About 5 minutes per game

Equipment: None

> You need a sheet of A4 paper, a pen and something to lean the paper on for this addictive game that adults find therapeutic too (well, I do).

> Draw a grid of dots – I normally draw one 7 x 5 to play this game with one child, but do more dots if there are more of you. The youngest starts to connect one dot with another, then everyone takes it in turns. The idea of the game is to be the one to finish the most boxes, i.e. close the fourth line.

> The lucky guy or gal to finish a box gets to put their initials in the box and also gets the next go. It gets pretty exciting towards the end, let me tell you, when there are no safe options left…

'Knock, Knock' Jokes

Number of children needed: One–lots

Age group: 5–80 years old

Preparation and energy required from grown-up: None

Duration: 5 minutes

Equipment: None

Personally, and perhaps a bit tragically, I like the ones that work with real names and real door situations! But the more surreal and illogical, the funnier for children. Adding 'Let me in, Muppet!' at the end gives my daughter the giggles. When you are done with these, get them to make their own jokes up and be prepared for both the painful and the hilarious.

Knock, knock.
Who's there?

Mikey.
Mikey who?
My key doesn't work! Let me in, Muppet!

Anita...
I need to use your loo! Let me in, Muppet!

Howard...
I heard you were having a party! Let me in, Muppet!

Theodore...
The door doesn't open! Let me in, Muppet!

Cher...
(American accent required) Sure would
be nice if you let me in, Muppet!

Luke...
Look through the keyhole and you'll
see me! Let me in, Muppet!

Olivia...
I live here, not you! Go away, Muppet!

Silly Jokes

Number of children needed: One–lots

Age group: 5–10 years old

Preparation and energy required from grown-up: None

Duration: 5 minutes

Equipment: None

Where do pencils go on holiday?

Pennsylvania.

Why is six afraid of seven?

Because seven eight nine.

When is cheese not your cheese?

When it's Nacho cheese.

How can you make a hanky dance?

When you put a boogey in it.

Doctor, can I have a cream to get rid of my spots?

I can't make any rash decisions.

What do you call a penguin in the jungle?

Lost.

What do you call a penguin at the top of a tree?

High.

What do you call a man with a spade in his head?

Doug.

What do you call a man without a spade in his head?

Douglas.

Riddles

Number of children needed: One–lots

Age group: 6–12 years old

Preparation and energy required from grown-up: None

Duration: 10 minutes

Equipment: None

Question	Answer
What has a face and two hands, but no arms or legs?	A clock.
What is the easiest way to double your money?	Put it in front of the mirror.
What has a thumb and four fingers, but is not alive?	A glove.
What has to be broken before you can use it?	An egg.

What has a neck but no head?	A bottle.
What gets wetter as it dries?	A towel.
What goes up and doesn't come back down?	Your age.
What belongs to you, but is used more by others?	Your name.
Everyone has it and no one can lose it, what is it?	A shadow.
It's been around for millions of years, but it's no more than a month old. What is it?	The Moon.

Lateral-Thinking Games

Number of children needed: One–lots

Age group: 6–10 years old

Preparation and energy required from grown-up: None

Duration: 15 minutes

Equipment: None

Question	Answer
There are six eggs in a basket. Six people each take one of the eggs. How can it be that one egg is left in the basket?	The last person took the basket as well as the last egg.
Acting on an anonymous phone call, the police raid a house where they have been told everyone is playing a card game. They want to arrest a 'naughty man'. They don't know what he looks like but they know his name is John and that he is inside the house.	

The police bust in on a carpenter, a lorry driver, a mechanic and a fireman – all playing poker. Without hesitation or communication of any kind, they immediately arrest the fireman. How do they know they've got their naughty man?

The others were all women.

A cowboy arrives in town on Friday. He stays for three nights and then leaves on Friday. Explain.

His horse is called Friday.

A man walks into a bar and asks the barman for a glass of water. The barman pours a glass of water, but suddenly pulls out a gun and points it at the man. The man says thank you and leaves. Why?

He had hiccups.

Five pieces of coal, a carrot and a scarf are lying on the lawn. Nobody put them on the lawn but there is a perfectly logical reason why they are there. What is it?

A snowman has melted.

A woman had two sons who were born on the same hour of the same day of the same year, but they were not twins. How could this be possible?	She had triplets – the other one was a girl.
A woman was pushing her car. She stopped pushing when she reached a hotel and then realised she was bankrupt. Why?	She was playing Monopoly.
A man died and went to heaven. He saw thousands of people there, all naked and young. He saw a couple and he immediately recognised them as Adam and Eve. How did he know?	They had no tummy buttons.

Fun In Tunnels (Car Journeys)

Number of children needed: One–lots

Age group: 5–7 years old

Preparation and energy required from grown-up: None

Duration: Depends on the tunnels!

Equipment: None

> Kids aged 5–7 love this little game. When you approach a tunnel, count down from three. On arrival in the tunnel everybody has to hold their breath until the end, or as long as they can. Winner is the one with the reddest face! Bonus for grown-ups is that it creates a lovely silence when the tunnels are nice and long.

> If you are in a congested area, try it between traffic lights, parents with prams, people wearing hats, people on bicycles, etc.

Hum That Tune

Number of children needed: One–lots

Age group: 6–10 years old

Preparation and energy required from grown-up: None

Duration: 10 minutes or longer if you are having fun!

Equipment: None

> Take turns to hum tunes until the other passengers guess the song. From Christmas carols, 'Wheels On The Bus', 'Heads, Shoulders, Knees and Toes' – to of course the rather easy 'Let It Go'. Also, use your phone to start songs with strong lyrics then press pause and see if anyone can guess the next word in the song.

Spell Your Destination

Number of children needed: One–lots

Age group: 6–12 years old

Preparation and energy required from grown-up: None

Duration: Depends on how populated with signs and other cars your journey is, and how many letters the name of your destination has!

Equipment: None

> Each passenger in the car needs to spot letters from billboards, licence plates and signs to spell out the name of their destination.

> Half the players are allowed to look out to the left, and the other half to the right. All players are allowed to look ahead and behind.

> The first player to have noted down all the letters that spell out the destination to which they are headed is the winner. Obviously, this is for over six year olds, and not for when you are on a terrible holiday in the Gobi Desert.

Find The Alphabet

Number of children needed: One–lots

Age group: 7–12 years old (good spellers)

Preparation and energy required from grown-up: Getting the kids to write out the alphabet before the journey and providing pens

Duration: 15 minutes

Equipment: None

> Spell the whole alphabet. The little passengers must write out the whole alphabet before the car journey begins. Then they have to find something that begins with each letter (in no particular order).

> They can either look out of the window only, or you can allow things inside the car if you want a faster game, or in alphabetical order if you want a longer game. Massive points for Q and Z (which can be ignored of course) but X should be seen at an EXIT sign fairly quickly.

> The first player to fill in their alphabet sheet is of course victorious!

Last-Letter Game

> **Number of children needed:** One–lots
>
> **Age group:** 8–12 years old
>
> **Preparation and energy required from grown-up:** None
>
> **Duration:** 5 minutes per category
>
> **Equipment:** None

This game is for older children that can spell, obviously.

> Somebody comes up with a category, such as animals, food, countries, characters from TV or film.

> The youngest player starts with an example (say, elephant), and the next person clockwise has to come up with another animal beginning with the last letter from elephant. And so on.

> Anyone who can't come up with anything after approximately 15 seconds is eliminated. It is amazing how flummoxed one can be under pressure!

Bingo On The Road

Number of children needed: One–lots

Age group: 6–10 years old

Preparation and energy required from grown-up: Creating bingo cards before you leave. It will take you five minutes to create each card.

Duration: Depends how busy the roads are!

Equipment: None

> This one needs a tiny bit of preparation before you leave the house in that you must design a bingo card for each potentially bored little traveller. You need three or more players for this game to work well, plus an adult (ideally not driving…) to be the bingo caller.

> So each card (or sheet of paper with a book to rest it on) should have nine squares, with double numbers in each square (from ten up to 99). Each card must of course have totally different numbers.

> When you hear the first plaintive cry of 'are-we-nearly-there-yet?' hand out the cards and pens. The adult playing the bingo caller now starts the game by looking for number plates and calling out two-digit numbers.

Whoever has them on their card puts a big cross over that box.

> You can either declare the winner the first player who has a row of numbers crossed out, or the marathon version for really long journeys can be the winner is the first player to have crossed off all their numbers.

Bingo On The Road With Words

> As 'Bingo On the Road', but fill in the cards with words that you think the children might see on their journey, for example stop, exit, supermarket, restaurant, toilets, slow, petrol, miles, historic market town, beach, town centre, school, hospital, taxi, car park, dead end, etc.!

(You can play bingo with numbers and words at the same time. Less monotonous but they will need two smaller cards that they can work with on their laps, supported by a book, at the same time.)

The Name Game

Number of children needed: One–lots

Age group: 7– 12 years old

Preparation and energy required from grown-up: Writing down names of famous people everybody in the car will know, and putting each name in a box or hat, folded up

Duration: Depends on how many people are playing but roughly 20 minutes

Equipment: None

As an adult, this is an absolute favourite of mine. It is simply the best dinner party game ever. Some of you will know it as a round they used to do years ago on *Have I Got News For You?*, but it can be a lot of fun on long car or plane journeys with children too.

> Some preparation is required before you set off, and to set this game up you need to have a good understanding of which famous characters or people the kids will know.

> To play the game you need one or more pairs. It requires children to be able to read names and to read quite well, so they need to be 9 years old or over.

> Write down as many famous names as you can that your lot will know. Father Christmas, The Easter Bunny, Mickey Mouse, Donald Duck, Elsa, Anna or Olaf from *Frozen*, Marshall, Chase, Sky etc. from *Paw Patrol*, Twilight and Sparkle from *My Little Pony*, Suzi, Danny, Peppa from *Peppa Pig*. You get the drift. Now write the names on pieces of paper and fold them so they can't be seen. Put them in a box or a hat.

> Start a stopwatch on your phone and set it for two minutes. In each round one person grabs a piece of paper, opens it up, reads it, and begins to describe the character to their partner WITHOUT SAYING THE NAME OR ANY PART OF THE NAME.

> So, if you got the piece of paper that says Father Christmas, you would say 'He brings presents on the 25th of December. He is old and has a white beard'. You would not be able to say 'he brings presents at Christmas' because Christmas is part of his name. This is a good example to show them how to play.

> When the partner has guessed a name, one point is scored for the person describing (the skill is in the describing, NOT the guessing!) then another name is grabbed until the time is up.

> If several pairs are playing then the scores are tallied when all the names have been used. If one pair is playing the person who got the most points for their descriptions wins.

Don't Say Yes Or No!

Number of children needed: One–lots

Age group: 6–10 years old

Preparation and energy required from grown-up: None

Duration: 15 minutes or the whole journey if you dare!

Equipment: None

> Simple game, ideal for journeys where you chat with each other and try to make the other people say 'yes' or 'no'. If they do, they are out. My daughter loves to catch people out by asking what people make when it snows (a sNOwman) or what they did 24 hours ago (YESterday…).

> It's a cute game where children (over six years old) get to practise the evasive language skills and diplomacy that us adults have developed for better or worse!

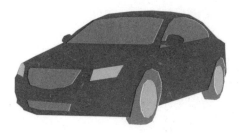

Scissors, Paper, Stone

Number of children needed: One–lots

Age group: 6–10 years old

Preparation and energy required from grown-up: None

Duration: 5 minutes

Equipment: None

> This is an absolute classic. Each person shakes their hands three times behind their back and then presents their hand in the form of either a stone (clenched fist), paper (flat palm) or scissors (first finger and second finger wide). The winner each time is the person whose hand is deemed the strongest. Paper wraps stone, so wins over stone; scissors cut paper, so wins over paper; and stone smashes scissors. So each winning hand gets a point.

(This is also a good way of determining who goes first in any game.)

Odds And Evens

Number of children needed: One–lots

Age group: 6–10 years old

Preparation and energy required from grown-up: None

Duration: 10 minutes

Equipment: None

This is a bit like 'Scissors, Paper, Stone' but they might not know this one.

> Divide into two teams, with one team being ODD and the other team EVEN. They will need to be aged over 6 to get this.

> Players take it in turns to shout out 'one, two, three, GO!' and everyone throws out a few fingers from one hand.

> Add up the fingers on both teams. If the number is odd the ODD team gets a point; if it's even, the EVEN team gets a point.

> After ten goes, add up the points. And then play something else!

Gloves And Sweets (Or Chewing Gum)

Number of children needed: One–lots

Age group: 6–10 years old

Preparation and energy required from grown-up: Sourcing gloves for each player and some wrapped sweets or chewing gum

Duration: 5 minutes

Equipment: None

A silly bit of fun to kill a few minutes in a car if you have kids' gloves (not metaphorically) or, even better, mittens that you don't mind potentially getting a bit sticky in the interests of a few giggles.

> Put the gloves or mittens on the minions and give them each at the same time a piece of chewing gum or a sweet to unwrap. First one to do so wins.

> When they have finished the sweet or chewing gum, if they enjoyed it, start again.

> (At least when they are eating or chewing you hear less 'are-we-nearly-there-yet?'…)

Draw Family Trees

Number of children needed: One–lots

Age group: 6–10 years old

Preparation and energy required from grown-up: Providing paper and pens and something to lean on per player

Duration: Depends on the size of your family!

Equipment: None

> Give each offspring a blank piece of A4 paper. Briefly describe how a family tree works.

> Take turns Mum and Dad, to describe who was married to who in your families, who had which kids and what the aunties, uncles and cousins are called.

> The player with the tree most correctly drawn at the next motorway services wins and gets to make a call to the family member they are most curious about. (Hehehehehe!)

Mr & Mrs

Number of children needed: One–lots (but two parents!)

Age group: 7–12 years old

Preparation and energy required from grown-up: None

Duration: 20 minutes

Equipment: None

> This game works best if there is a happy Mum and Dad as part of the family! If so, the little ones will love feeling part of that love, being very nosey and testing their parents' devotion to each other!

> If you are a single parent but have more than one child you could play this game too, testing out how well the siblings know each other.

> In the classic game, the kids come up with five questions for Mum about Dad and five questions for Dad about Mum. One parent's answers are not disclosed until the other parent has guessed!

> So to begin: kids ask the questions, Mum writes her answers, Dad has to answer verbally.

> Points are then scored for which answers Dad got right as the kids read out Mum's answers! Dad is up next (but preferably not while driving!).

Suggested questions for Dad about Mum!

> What is Mummy's favourite ice cream flavour?

> What is Mummy's star sign?

> What does Mummy get most cross with Daddy about?

> Who is Mummy's favourite singer?

> What is Mummy's favourite drink?

> Who would Mummy rather kiss: Father Christmas, Daddy or George Clooney?

> The way to play this in a car, is to get Mum to play first. Ladies first after all.

Suggested questions for Mum about Dad!

> Who is Daddy's favourite football player?

> What was the name of Daddy's first ever girlfriend?

> What does Daddy get most cross about Mummy doing?

> Would Daddy prefer a trip to a football match or a romantic dinner with Mummy and if so which restaurant?

> What is Daddy's least favourite job around the house?

> Which meal that Mummy cooks does Daddy not like very much?

Bonkers Language

Number of children needed: One–lots

Age group: 6–10 years old

Preparation and energy required from grown-up: None

Duration: 20 minutes or the whole journey if you dare!

Equipment: None

> Everyone in the car, train or plane has to come up with five new words for things that the family normally talks about or that they can see.

> For example, ours might be: 'Blakkavah' for car; 'Eeko' for water; 'Neenah' for no; 'Wishywishy' for yes.

> Players take it in turns to announce their new words and teach them to the others.

> Let the conversations and questions, in particular, begin.

> One conversation might be 'Tell me what you did today before you got in the car'. Another might be 'Describe your last birthday party'. Another might be 'What can you see out of the window?'

> The other players are free to 'butt in' with questions at any time.

> Anyone who forgets a new bit of vocab is penalised by a point.

> The winner is the person with the least penalty points after 15 minutes.

About the Author

Fiona Jennison is devoted to the art of fun and games. She worked in the television industry in the UK for many years, getting paid to film all sorts of silly stuff, sometimes with somewhat famous comedians. Eventually this meant that she could get a mortgage on a boat, allowing her to move to the permanent playground of Ibiza, where after a bit more paperwork she managed to get paid for taking people sailing. Following the unexpected arrival of her first and last child eight years ago, Fiona retrained as an English language teacher and has since worked with hundreds of Spanish children, constantly coming up with new games to make learning English more fun. These ideas – as well as the depressing sight of children on holiday with their eyes glued to electronic gadgets – gradually gave birth to this collection of games. Fiona has never worked harder in her life and probably never will again.

If you're interested in finding out
more about our books, find us on Facebook
at Summersdale Publishers and follow
us on Twitter at @Summersdale

www.summersdale.com